Peer Mediation

≈ ≈

DUTY

Fool, do not beat the air
  With miserable hands—
The wrong is done, the seed is sown,
  The evil stands.

Your duty is to draw
  Out of the web of wrong,
Out of ill-woven deeds,
  A thread of song.

Sara Teasdale

Peer Mediation

≈ ≈

Finding a Way to Care

Judith M. Ferrara

Stenhouse Publishers
York, Maine

Stenhouse Publishers, 226 York Street, York, Maine 03909

Library of Congress Cataloging-in-Publication Data

Ferrara, Judith M., 1942–
    Peer mediation : finding a way to care / Judith M. Ferrara.
        p.   cm.
    Includes bibliographical references (p.   ).
    ISBN 1-57110-021-0 (alk. paper)
    1. Peer counseling of students—Social aspects—United States—
Case studies.   2. Conflict management—Study and teaching
(Elementary)—Social aspects—United States—Case studies.
3. Educational anthropology—United States—Case studies.   I. Title.
LB1027.5.F46   1996
371.4'6—dc20   96-15507
                                                             CIP

Cover and interior design by Joyce C. Weston
Typeset by Technologies 'N Typography

Manufactured in the United States of America on acid-free paper

99 98 97 96 8 7 6 5 4 3 2 1

*I dedicate this book
to my husband, John,
with my love
and appreciation.*

CONTENTS

ACKNOWLEDGMENTS

It always seemed odd to me that acknowledgments are placed at the beginning of a book because I know that they cannot be written until a writer's long journey is nearly over. After all, how can a writer know whom to thank before first testing the patience, knowledge, love, or friendship of many people by writing a book?

Whenever I begin reading a book, I often wonder who these people are. I know that writers need to pay tribute, to reach out their hands, to touch people who helped them in some way.

I am no different. I hear the rhythm of these names and recognize the heartbeat of this book. For each name that appears on this page, silent movies begin in my mind. Subtitles flash under scenes in which each person displayed specific qualities—encouragement, support, faith, confidence, help, love, concern, curiosity, humor. Thank you.

Jennie and David Benigas. Michael Breault. Joe and Chris Hay. Lucille Cormier. Al and Barbara Schifferle. Victor and Esther Ferrara. Rita Ferrara. Agnes and Will LaHiff. Emmy Broomfield. Dorrie and Dick Daigle. Evelyn and Amy Beth Taublieb. Scott Gaumond.

George and Beth Miller. Helen O'Flaherty. Ron Colbert. Patricia Barbaresi. Robert Tapply. Vincent and Clare Mara. Franz Nowotny. JoAnn Pellecchia. Bill Strader. Michele Moran Zide.

Liana Kolb. Melinda Persons. Vicky Considine. Laurie DeRosa. Carmelita Hoffman. Joe Renda. Lance Johnson. Debbie Turner. Carol Ryan. Nick Quaratiello. Philip Fallon. Diane Rouleau.

Donald Murray. Donald Graves. Jane Hansen. Tom Newkirk. Pat Sullivan. Paula Flemming. Pearl Rosenberg. Tom Schram. Ann Diller. John Carney. Bert Feintuch.

Special appreciation goes to Philippa Stratton, a gifted editor.

My husband, John Gaumond, to whom this book is dedicated, has been my main source of support and encouragement, as well as my first reader.

And to my mother, Josephine—a special acknowledgment for supplying me with her special brand of tenacity.

SECTION ONE

≈≈≈≈≈≈≈≈≈≈≈≈≈≈≈≈≈≈≈≈≈≈≈≈

Before Starting a Peer Mediation Program

CHAPTER ONE

≈ ≈

Toward Resolving Conflicts in Hampton Campus School

We're in Trouble

That was the message written on the faces of both fifth-grade boys slumped silently in chairs facing the assistant principal's desk. It was a sunny October day in 1992. Danny Rodriguez shifted his thin frame away from his opponent to face the solitary window. He looked outside as groups of Riverton State College students drifted toward their 9:30 classes in C wing, which was off-limits to campus school students. Each boy told Mr. Reynolds his side of the dispute that had brought them there and, together, they agreed to the facts. A pro-social action report (see Appendix A.1) would now be used to document their inappropriate behavior. Jamie Caron's brown eyes slid from the white tiled floor to Mr. Reynolds' computer and saw their description of the feud play chase with the cursor on the blue screen, while Danny continued to gaze toward the window.

> **Hampton Campus School Pro-Social Action Report**
>
> *Situation* (What happened?): Danny and Jamie started to call each other names in class. Each of them says the other started it. The name-calling escalated into a fistfight that each says the other started.
>
> *Problem/s:* Neither of these boys was doing what they were supposed to be doing.
>
> *Solution:* Please speak to your child about name-calling and fighting.
>
> *Consequence:* They will lose their lunch recess today.

Mr. Reynolds said, "Both of you will take one copy of this to your teacher and bring the other one home and show it to your parents. I will be mailing a third copy to them." He sent them back to class, satisfied that they had talked out their problem, seen it recorded and added to the school's disciplinary data base, and had time to consider the consequences of their violent behavior during their lost recess. Mr. Reynolds described this process to me in an interview and added, "I don't send them [the letters] home so the child will be punished.

(Author's note: Pseudonyms are used for each participant, as well as the location described. All students selected their own pseudonyms.)

They're punished here. But I do want their parents talking to them, letting them know what their expectations are."

How might Danny and Jamie view the assistant principal's letter? They knew from experience that it was only a matter of time before a printout of their dispute would begin a journey destined to end in their parents' hands. That might mean double trouble if their parents' reaction was to mete out more punishment, *unless* they could intercept the mail and effectively block their parents' participation in this conflict.

Danny and Jamie were in a bind. They had ostensibly paid the price for their wrongdoing (the lost recess), but Mr. Reynolds believed that part of the solution rested with their parents' becoming informed about it. He assumed that parental support was necessary to Hampton's pro-social discipline process and included an explanation in the cover letter attached to each report:

> When a problem is referred to the office, regardless of where it occurred, all the parties get together to discuss the situation, the problem, and the solution and to determine the consequence. The content of the discussion is typed on a form (attached). Copies are then sent to the referring teacher, the homeroom teacher, the guidance counselor, and the parent(s).

Communication with other adults seemed to be a high priority for Jim Reynolds. However, Danny and Jamie might be compelled to choose the lesser of two evils: punishment for getting into trouble at school or punishment for getting caught intercepting the mail.

During an interview, Jim Reynolds told me that "less than 20 or 25 percent" of his pro-social action reports were signed and returned by parents (see Appendix A.1). When I asked him what he thought about the remaining 75 or 80 percent, he said,

> In some cases, it may be a child I have seen once. If it's a child I've seen ten to fifteen times, then I wonder . . . If I talk with parents of a repeat offender, then I go through the data base and say, "I sent one on this date and on this date." We used to send them out in Riverton State College envelopes. Now we wait a few days and send them out in blank envelopes to try to confuse students. Some of them are slick. They have the job of getting the mail, so they can intercept anything. If they're in trouble only once or twice, then I don't worry about it. If they say, "I'm not going to get in trouble any more because my mom will find out," then GREAT, if that's what keeps them out of trouble.

Jim Reynolds seemed to see students' fear of parents' retribution as a positive feature if it worked to keep students under control while they were in school. I wondered about the risk they were taking by intercepting mail from Hampton Campus School and calculated the high price they could be paying to play this game, namely, fear, deceit, and guilt. It reminded me of a note that Robert Coles' wife wrote to him while he was writing *The Moral Life of Children:*

> Children receive all kinds of moral signals, and they have to figure out which ones to consider important and which ones to ignore. Sometimes

they can't ignore what they've decided they'd better try and ignore, and then they're in a jam. (Coles 1986, p. 8)

To begin considering Hampton's system of discipline, it was necessary to view it from both a student's perspective and an administrator's. Jim Reynolds' role as assistant principal meant that he was responsible for handling the school's discipline. His experience in dealing with students who had conflicts that ended in physical violence seemed to have an effect on the way he interpreted events outside Hampton's walls.

Four months later, we stood in the corridor outside his office and talked about the morning's headlines: "Hotel worker beaten to death—Riverton man pleads not guilty." The victim was Peter Lindell, a twenty-two-year-old Anglo-American Riverton State business major who came from the next town. Accused was Andrew Forman, a twenty-four-year-old African American who grew up a few blocks away and attended the campus school junior high more than a decade before. His photo brought to mind a well-behaved student who earned average grades in my English class. The regional newspaper described from several points of view what took place in the parking lot of the hotel where they both worked:

> Forman . . . instigated the fight, spitting in Lindell's face and taunting him, according to Assistant District Attorney James Vacare. The prosecutor did not say what caused the fight, but he said it ended with Forman pounding Lindell's head against the pavement . . . Witnesses to the fight . . . said that [Lindell] was defending a woman being harassed by Forman in the parking lot. When he intervened, Lindell became the target of the fight.

Jim Reynolds shook his head and said, "When I read how it happened, it was exactly what the kids do, just like my reports. You have a conflict, one person says something to another person, and they give a hit. Of course, they took it further. I tell these kids: once you put your hands on someone, you have no idea where that's going to take you. You don't know. The key is, keep your hands off." I nodded in agreement because I saw in Mr. Reynolds' reaction the leap over time he was making: students who cannot control violent responses to conflict become adults who kill or injure others. I thought back to Danny and Jamie and wondered what other solutions they might have considered before their fists started flying. What other strategies had they and other students acquired to help them resolve a conflict?

I asked myself these questions because I planned to begin a peer mediation program in Hampton Campus School as part of a research project for my doctoral dissertation (Ferrara 1994), and intended to continue as coordinator/trainer thereafter as part of my teaching load in the education department.

I needed to learn all that I could about conflicts in this pre-K through grade 5 school before starting a program. Between September 4, 1992, and June 18, 1993, Jim Reynolds shared 351 discipline reports with me. Reading them each day was like running my bare hand along barbed wire—hitting, slapping, scratching, punching, shoving, pinching, kicking. Violence stemmed from racist, homophobic, or sexist insults (chink, nigger, fag, bimbo, bitch) or revenge ("That's for telling on me,") or responses to exclusion from a play group or to teasing about a new haircut. The children involved were usually between eight and eleven years old. Even though I was nearing my thirtieth year as a teacher and had arbitrated countless arguments and broken up my share of fights, these narratives still had a chilling effect on me.

In May, Danny was suspended in-school for the remainder of the year for bringing two knives into the building. He told his teacher and Mr. Reynolds that he had them for protection from the posse in the neighborhood. The principal, Dr. Richard Camden, sent a letter to parents:

> As you may have heard, this week a youngster was found to have two knives in his possession on school property. His intention was not to harm anyone. However, we have suspended him indefinitely until a final decision is taken by the Superintendent's office.
>
> While it may seem self-evident that students are not to carry a dangerous instrument on school property, I must inform you of School Committee Policy #510.
>
> IF A STUDENT CARRIES A DANGEROUS INSTRUMENT ONTO SCHOOL PROPERTY, THEN SAID STUDENT WILL BE IMMEDIATELY SUSPENDED AND REFERRED TO AN EXPULSION HEARING BEFORE THE SUPERINTENDENT AND THE SCHOOL COMMITTEE.

Danny was suspended in-house until the last day of school. He reported to the office first thing in the morning and received schoolwork provided by his teacher. He ate his lunch in the administrator/office staff coffee room. Danny punctuated the isolation of his school day by interrupting secretaries with requests. "Can I help you? Can I call my mother? Can I ask Mr. Reynolds if I can go to the bathroom?" When they complained to Mr. Reynolds that Danny was disturbing them, he was sent across the hall to the guidance counselor's office. But Clare Riley would send him back to the main office when she had to deal with other student issues privately. Danny now attends the middle school several blocks away.

Now It's Part of My Life

I press down on the right turn signal and pull into Hampton's parking lot. I notice Carol Avelon letting her son off at the front door. I remember her as a quiet seventh-grade student with a droll sense of humor. Seeing her this morning pushes me gently back in time. I began teaching in 1964 at an elementary school in Buffalo, New York. However, my professional life has been tied to this campus school in New England since it opened in January 1971. I have lived and loved (for the most part) my teacher's life inside the squat, red brick building. I started as a junior high school English teacher in C wing. Then, in 1978, a reduction in the city's enrollment eliminated the campus school's seventh, eighth, and ninth grades, so I taught third and fourth grades in A wing. In 1987 I became a member of the education department, which has its offices in Hampton's B wing.

During the time I took to pursue further graduate studies, I chose to observe a community-based mediation program as a project site for a research methods course. It was a choice that affected my future more than I could have anticipated (see Chapter 4). I became a mediator and decided to begin a peer mediation program with elementary students and look at ways they used language to understand the process. The experience was the basis of my dissertation study, as well as the foundation of this book. Because of my belief in the process and my commitment to the students, parents, teachers, and administrators, I continue today as coordinator/coach in Hampton's program.

In the fall of 1992, I began a yearlong process of implementing a peer mediation program because I believed that students could learn to help each other resolve conflicts peacefully. Elaine Lindquist, a fifth-grade student who was a volunteer peer mediator during the first two years of Hampton's program, expressed it this way: "It's bigger than I thought it was. Last year, peer mediation wouldn't even have crossed my mind. Now it's part of my life." Peer mediation is designed to empower students to help each other resolve conflicts without the presence or intervention of adults. This book is about how Elaine and others in Hampton Campus School's community added a new Discourse to their repertoire of identities: daughter or son, student, gymnast, cheerleader, soccer player, computer technician, *peer mediator.*

Sociolinguist James Gee (1990) described the Discourse "tools" of culture as "values, attitudes, gestures . . . ways of talking, writing, acting, interacting, [and] thinking" (p. 171). I noticed during my training that mediation Discourse is played out in a prescribed form and order—introduction, joint sessions, mediator caucuses, negotiated agreements, and conclusions. Mediators and disputants learn a set of norms for participating in a mediation.

- Be honest.
- Agree to try to work on the problem.
- Agree to no name-calling or interrupting.

They use a set of norms to assess an agreement. Is it specific? Does it share responsibility? Are both disputants able to do what they promise? Are the solutions permanent? Mediation offers a large vocabulary of terms, skills, and strategies: confidentiality, voluntariness, neutrality, trust, empathy, emotions, body language, dispute, agreement, brainstorming, and active listening. Participation in a peer mediation program means that a group of students will acquire a unique and potentially powerful Discourse.

A Higher Literacy

If you are an advocate of students and are about to become involved in a peer mediation program, this book is intended as a guide to help you explore and appreciate the potent experiences you will certainly have. If you are currently involved in a budding or established program, then what you might learn from Hampton Campus School students could cause you to confirm, contradict, or rethink some of what you already know.

The National Association for Mediation in Education/National Institute for Dispute Resolution (see Appendix A.6) is an organization that serves as a clearinghouse for manuals and materials that support the burgeoning interest in school-based mediation. Each year, more publishers are responding to the demand that a trend in conflict resolution is creating (see Appendix A.2). However, there is very little written by educators who have had a long-term experience. This book offers insights that more than three years as a peer mediation program coordinator/coach and researcher have given me. It is intended to encourage you to understand, design, implement, and revise your peer mediation program by learning about one program that is described in detail. It sustains a narrative that includes several points of view. Hampton's students, teachers, administrators, and parents interacted with me and lend their voices to this project.

This book should not be construed as a program evaluation. It does not represent an outside evaluator's perspective, but a participant observer's. My purpose is not to show how this mediation program affected a school's rate of violent incidents or suspensions, although that information is woven into the text. It is not a gathering of perceptions about changes in a school's climate or in peer mediators' self-esteem, even though that, too, finds a place within these pages. It is an effort to share lessons that these fourth- and fifth-grade students taught me about the meanings that grew from having a peer mediation program in their school. I believe that these important basic lessons can be applied to elementary, middle, and secondary mediation programs.

What makes this account different from other studies or books about peer mediation that you may read is its primary attention to the students' perspectives, especially those of the peer mediation volunteers. You will read about how they worked within a program model and engaged in what Donald Graves described as "a higher literacy [that included] 'problem finding' as one of its components" (Brown 1991, p. 34). Regular discussions enabled them to identify and try to solve problems within the program. With that came in-depth learning about the mediation process and their role within it.

I believe it is important to document these events and perceptions by exploring the meanings that the *students* conferred on individual words and acts. Why? The most crucial reason is conveyed in this vignette from *The Call of Service: A Witness to Idealism* by Robert Coles (1993). In the early 1970s, he became involved with a group of parents and teachers from a predominantly Black community in Massachusetts who "had decided to remove their children from Roxbury's terribly overcrowded schools and send them elsewhere in hopes of securing a better education" (p. 14). These students shared a common purpose with peer mediators today: they were volunteers who were trying to make a difference. Coles wrote about one girl who talked of "the social and economic disparities that bothered her." She said to Coles: "'There's a lot riding on you kids,' some of those people say, but it's *us* who are *doing* it, the *riding* . . ." (p. 29). Her statement meant this to me: students who become mediators need the careful attention and support of knowledgeable teachers, guidance counselors, parents, and administrators. Whenever we point to them with pride, it seems important not to forget that it is they who are doing "the riding."

To help you understand the Hampton Campus School experience, this book is divided into three sections:

> Section One, "Before Starting a Peer Mediation Program," focuses on key understandings and experiences that provided a foundation for beginning a program.

Section Two, "Starting Up a Peer Mediation Program," is a documentation of events during the first six months of Hampton's program.

Section Three, "Maintaining a Peer Mediation Program," examines factors that affected the program over time.

Each of the twelve chapters include four elements: vignettes that demonstrate what it means to be a part of Hampton's community and peer mediation program; information about mediation theory and research, as well as strategies that helped me initiate and sustain the school's program; recommendations that grew out of my experience; and sets of questions that are intended to guide you through each phase in developing and maintaining a successful program.

Chapter 2: Understand Your School's Culture

Peer mediation programs are like liquids that take the shape of their containers; they can look quite different from one another because each is socially situated in its own school's culture. Chapter 2 considers the necessity of first understanding how students perceive themselves in school and how they are perceived by adults as contributing members of the school/community. The use of conflict resolution curriculum as a foundation for introducing a peer mediation program is examined from student and staff perspectives. The chapter describes how conflicts were managed in Hampton Campus School and argues for the need to understand conflict resolution patterns at work in a school's culture before program implementation.

Chapter 3: Understand Your Community's Culture

Jerome Bruner (1990) suggested that "the viability of a culture inheres in its capacity for resolving conflicts" (p. 47). If everyone trusted each other and resolved conflicts cooperatively and peacefully, then students' primary (home) and secondary (school and neighborhood) Discourses would be in harmony with mediation theory and practice. This chapter is built around discussions of three sources of conflict: threats to psychological and/or physical needs, resources, and culturally learned values. It offers a closer look at Riverton and considers how matches and mismatches between home, school, and community culture could impact a peer mediation program. Discussion is based on the understanding that all communities have conflicts and have attempted to resolve at least some of them. It considers how children witness conflicts within the community and what they might be learning from adults.

Chapter 4: Understand Mediation from the Inside

Mediation is a process that demands an understanding of a complex belief system, which presents the new learner with a set of five principles: self-determination, informed consent, confidentiality, neutrality, and voluntariness. This chapter is an exploration of my motivation to become trained as a mediator, as well as a description of that experience. It considers ethical and practical issues that surround varying levels of preparation for those intending to start programs in schools.

Chapter 5: Seeking Volunteers

How does a student learn what it means to volunteer to become a peer mediator? This chapter focuses on the use of a classroom presentation as a means of launching a program and examines the necessity of communicating with a school's staff and parents. It explores selection issues and considers how the act of volunteering might be interpreted in a school's culture.

Chapter 6: Selecting Peer Mediators

If the peer mediation model chosen is one in which a relatively small number of students are selected for training, then what are some ways in which that process can take place? This chapter explores issues that are embedded in this sensitive and complex part of the implementation process. It offers insights into what can be expected during various phases of the selection process, such as student nominations, interviews with volunteers, and selection meetings.

Chapter 7: Preparing Students to Mediate

What should peer mediators know before they sit down for their first mediation? What can a program coordinator/trainer expect to accomplish during an initial training? This chapter describes that experience and offers suggestions that are aimed at preparing a program coordinator/trainer to design the peer mediators' first immersion in their new role.

Chapter 8: Taking Hold

During the first days of the program, I overheard a fourth-grade student say to another student, "Hey, I'm a *pair* mediator! We're called that because we mediate in pairs." Listening in on what students are saying and carefully observing what they are doing helps coordinators to understand the meanings that students are constructing during the time of program implementation. This chapter stresses the need to read the signals students are sending with respect to how the program is taking hold in their culture. It also describes strategies that may be used to acquaint the school and community with peer mediation concepts.

Chapter 9: The Letter Home

Consciously or unconsciously, students constantly assess a peer mediation program as it becomes part of their school. In order to maintain a program, it is necessary for coordinators to encourage students to talk about its features and to demonstrate to them that their voices are being heard. This chapter describes how peer mediators worked to make one program change that occurred when disclosure of the mediated agreement became an issue powerful enough to keep students away from mediation.

Chapter 10: Program Changes: Finding and Solving Problems

Richard Cohen (1987a) cautioned others interested in implementing a peer mediation program:

> For every successful school mediation program functioning today, there is another program that has failed or is currently struggling to survive in

the face of serious difficulties. This is not because of deficiencies in the concept of mediation; rather the result of numerous obstacles which hinder the institutionalization of school mediation programs . . . the co-ordinators will more than likely find themselves "burned out" from the work they have been doing on their own time, and there will be few others in the school willing to take over their leadership roles . . . Extensive planning should . . . also be done to address such issues as funding, training needs (initial and on-going), coordination, scheduling and space. Finally, assistance from outside agencies should be pursued if it is available. (pp. 1, 3, 4)

When and where to schedule mediations is an early set of decisions a coordinator usually makes with an administrator's input and permission. Jim Reynolds allowed me to schedule mediations in the cafeteria during lunch periods and on the playground during recess. This chapter describes how peer mediators identified problems that resulted from these decisions and how their talk led to overcoming some of the obstacles mentioned by Cohen. It also looks at what it meant to peer mediators to carry out their role successfully.

When any problem is recognized and addressed, according to Cohen, change will necessarily be a part of the solution. The chapter discusses adjustments in Hampton's program related to funding, adult volunteer support, and the selection process.

Chapter 11: Peer Helpers: Finding Another Way to Care

Early in Hampton's peer mediation program, fourth-grade mediator Sean Boudreau talked with me about what it meant to be part of a new group dedicated to helping students solve conflicts:

> I would be happy to help by talking about a problem if it's at home, at school, wherever it is. We're really here for school problems, but if kids shut down, and they don't want to talk at home about it, then they can talk about it with us. We don't tell them what to do to solve the problem, but we kind of guide them through. We're not going to be like their parents and boss them around. We're going to make them figure it out for themselves because then they can use what they learned at another time in a later conflict.

Sean believed that the importance of his newly acquired role lay in being available to his peers and that helping students solve their own problems with guidance during mediation could benefit them in the future. His words, grounded in an ethic of caring, contained the seeds of a new role created by another generation of Hampton's peer mediators. Three years later, Sean had moved on to middle school, and a different crop of mediators recognized their desire to help *individual* students who were having interpersonal and intrapersonal problems that were not necessarily appropriate for mediation. This chapter describes how they designed the role of peer helper in an effort to reach out to students who needed someone their own age to help them talk about their problems. However, it was a role that produced tension between their belief in mediation's principle of self-determination and their desire to give advice.

Chapter 11 also brings up an ethical issue: the need for caution on the part of responsible adults when preparing peer helpers and help seekers for participation in an interaction that could mean disclosure of sensitive personal information.

Chapter 12: What's It For?

What can it mean to maintain a peer mediation program? What good is it? What can people expect will happen in a school with a program? In order to understand possible answers to these questions, it is necessary to know whose perspective is being represented. This chapter uses the question "What's a peer mediation program for?" as a framework for exploring four points of view—that of administrator, teacher, program coordinator, and peer mediator.

A Step Back to Reflect

All through mediation training, my classroom teacher's voice insisted, "Kids need to do this." I believed that they could learn how to resolve conflicts, *without the presence of adults,* by using talk instead of resorting to violence or retreating from the problem in defeat. It made sense that once they developed those understandings and experiences at the individual level, there was a chance that they would view events in the larger community differently. The following interaction underlined that belief for me.

Hampton Campus School's program was five months old. John Grayson, a fifth-grade teacher, stopped at a neighborhood variety store. When he stepped into line to order two cold drinks to go, he noticed Ricky Villatoro, a peer mediator, waiting ahead of him. They started to talk when suddenly their conversation was overpowered by an argument escalating between a customer and the clerk behind the counter. Soon everyone's attention was riveted on the disputants as they argued over the woman's coffee order. Ricky looked up, smiled at Mr. Grayson and said, "Sounds like they might need a *mediator.*"

I believe that before the mediation program, Ricky might not have viewed this situation so objectively or, if he had, he would have chosen different words to finish his sentence: "Sounds like they might need a *referee.*" Or "Sounds like they might need a *lawyer.*"

This book is about the process that led Ricky to select the word "mediator." It is about Ricky and many other fourth- and fifth-grade students, whose ethic of caring about each other enabled them to risk creating a new role in school. It is about how these students answered the culture of violence and mistrust around them with an enduring and remarkable sense of community.

CHAPTER TWO

≈ ≈

Understand Your School's Culture

I'm Not in Trouble

John Grayson walked along the corridor toward the principal's office one morning and noticed six-year-old Nicole Santini standing beside the closed door of Miss Canton's first-grade classroom. John knew Nicole by name because his students worked there in book-buddy pairs and read together for a half an hour every Friday.

Nicole saw Mr. Grayson coming and anticipated his greeting with an immediate, fervent response: "I'm not in trouble. We're playing a game. I have to go in and find the ball they're hiding."

This vignette shows that a six-year-old had figured out how her presence in the hallway *might* be interpreted, and that she cared about setting Mr. Grayson straight. Nicole demonstrated her understanding of Hampton's culture as a practitioner of student Discourse in the sense that James Gee (1990) described it:

> Discourse is tied to a particular social identity within a particular social group and to certain social settings and institutions. Each is a *form of life*, a way of being in the world, a way of being 'a person like us', in terms of action, interaction, values, thought and language. (p. 174)

This interaction can be viewed from at least two perspectives. Mr. Grayson might have wondered what Nicole was doing out in the hall but did not think the worst. He knew from his experience in her classroom on alternating book-buddy weeks that Miss Canton did not use the hallway as a place reserved for time to think about unacceptable behavior. However, Nicole seemed not to trust that this fifth-grade teacher knew. Valuing her way of being perceived as a well-behaved student, she defended it through her explanation.

Mandy Arles, on the other hand, scowled at me and looked away when I tried to make eye contact with her as she slumped against the wall in the second-floor corridor. She had noticed me walking toward her fifth-grade classroom but, unlike Nicole, decided there was no need to explain her presence there. Her body language spoke loudly to passersby: she was involved in a conflict either with another student or the teacher and was biding her time until the door would open and Mr. Daiman would direct her to return.

Observing

Nicole's and Mandy's verbal and nonverbal language reflected their attitudes toward being perceived as "in trouble." It is crucial to take time to understand perspectives such as theirs *before* starting a peer mediation program, which empowers students to help each other resolve conflicts. It will be important to watch and listen to students and put yourself in their shoes. A starting point will be to develop strategies for understanding how students perceive themselves in relation to others within the routines of daily school life, that is, as practitioners of student Discourse:

> Discourses are ways of behaving, interacting, valuing, thinking, believing, speaking, and often reading and writing that are accepted as instantiations of particular roles by specific *groups of people* . . . They are always and everywhere *social* . . . Each of us is a member of many Discourses, and each Discourse represents one of our ever multiple identities. (Gee 1990, p. xix)

To understand that students are sensitive to where they are seen and by whom is to anticipate their acceptance of a process that requires them, as disputants, to voluntarily step into the role of problem solver.

Keep in mind that you will be trying to understand how students see themselves in various school settings and that this may be different from the ways adults see them. Frederick Erickson (1984) made the point that "teacher culture, administrator culture, and student culture may provide *cultural lenses* through which the same event looks different." I needed to step into Nicole's, Mandy's, Danny's, and Jamie's shoes before starting up a peer mediation program as a way of beginning to understand how they saw themselves practicing student Discourse and fitting into their school's culture. Experience with viewing situations from multiple perspectives is also germane to understanding the process of mediation (see Chapter 4).

Observer

A systematic look at your school's culture requires preparation. You will need to make arrangements to plan regular times for observing the school's routines. Your own direct observations of corridors, cafeteria, playground, and office areas should be brief but frequent, and should span several weeks.

If you are already a member of your school's community because you are a teacher, staff member, or administrator, then you will need to think about how your new role as an observer might be interpreted by others in the school. If you are not a member of your school's community, then you will need to think about how you will obtain permission to begin observations. Even though I had taught in the Hampton building since it opened in 1971, I had to renegotiate my entry. I had transferred from the campus school to the education department of Riverton State College in 1987 and, more recently, had taken a two-year leave to attend graduate school.

Early in September 1992, Dr. Richard Camden, Hampton's principal, allocated twenty minutes to me during his faculty meeting to talk about beginning the peer mediation project. Forty-five faculty and staff met in the library one day after school, and I talked with them about the several roles I would be taking on that would bring me back to Hampton Campus School—member of Riverton State College's education department, mediator, peer mediation program coordinator/trainer, and researcher. I had selected several handouts from the National Association for Mediation in Education's (NAME/NIDR) "Setting Up a Program: General Packet" (1991), designed to introduce the concept of peer mediation. At this point, I shared my time line: I would be taking at least two years to study and write about how children used language to understand the mediation process and would continue coordinating the program after the research ended:

> My project will focus on children's perceptions of what mediation means . . . When I watch them on the playground or in the hall, I want to see if I can observe instances of problem solving. Do they always approach you for help? In the cafeteria, when one student teases another, how does a student react to that? I'll be keeping a notebook to help me begin to figure out what's happening.

The teachers, staff, and administrators listened patiently. Several nodded in agreement when I spoke about the need to teach students strategies other than classic fight-or-flight patterns many used now to deal with conflict.

"Will this be for the primary grades, too?"

I told them about a study by psychologists Shure and Spivack (Meredith 1987) which showed that children as young as four years old could be taught conflict resolution techniques to reduce their aggressive behavior. I added that, from what I had read so far, students halfway through middle childhood find themselves on developmentally firm ground for involving themselves in the mediation process. By the age of eight or nine years, children's social development begins to favor stronger relationships with peers; their cognitive abilities develop as well, allowing them to follow an entire process and to understand others' perspectives (Piaget 1975). Therefore, by third or fourth grade, disputing students could be given the option of talking out conflicts with peers who are trained to take on the role of neutral third parties and help them develop a mutually satisfactory agreement (Davis and Porter 1985b).

"Are you going to do this in other schools also?"

I talked about meeting with Riverton's superintendent to discuss my focus on Hampton Campus School for this research study. Starting a pilot program with one school could result in a citywide plan, but it was too soon to tell.

An important aspect of this faculty meeting was that I began to connect with one group of adults so that they knew how to interpret my presence in their culture, Hampton Campus School. Like Nicole, I knew that it was necessary for me to do this, and it will be the same for you.

Observations

Once you begin a schedule of observations, you will need to find an effective way to use writing to anchor your experiences. I found that a double-entry notebook (Berthoff 1981) was most useful because it helped me to begin the task of examining Hampton Campus School's culture (Figure 2.1). The left side of the notebook was used for writing down details of what I saw and heard, verbatim quotations and drawings, sketches, or diagrams of each observation.

LEFT SIDE	RIGHT SIDE
9/1/92 - 11:00 a.m. Cafeteria 4 classrooms of fifth grade students take up about 3 of tables. Two teacher on duty. Students sit 12 at a table, waiting for MH (te.) to talk into the portable microphone. "Welcome back Good to see you again. In the cafeteria we show respect for each other, talk quietly, don't run. This year, you have only 20 minutes, not thirty, to eat your lunch. This year we need a volunteer from each table to wipe down each table." Three girls raised their hands. I asked JD how they knew what they were volunteering for. She said "That's the way we have always done it."	These students seem to know what to do in order to get along in this setting. The teacher with the microphone made certain to inform them of the much change (shortened lunch period) but the rest appeared to be "business as usual" with students knowing how to volunteer for a helping job. I'll have to find out if they get a reward (cookies?) for volunteering. And what do they give up? A few minutes of recess? When the noise level increased the heads down "command" was responded to with split second speed.

LEFT SIDE	RIGHT SIDE
volunteer got the cloth, wipe the tables, return the cloth." MH clicks on microphone. "Five minute warning. All trays back if you're finished or not." The noise level increases. "Heads down." All but a few of the 85 student assume a heads down position. Quickly. One boy was getting up to return his tray when he heard the "heads down" command. His face showed concern. Do I bring back my tray or put my head down? He did both: ducked his head while he walked toward the cafeteria counter	Even on the first day of school, they seemed to understand the consequences of not quieting down. So, what are they? JD's "That's the way we have always done it" is one student's way of figuring out the meaning of rituals: volunteering, heads down — The boy seemed to be caught between 2 ways of behaving: he needed to return his tray but also wanted to signal his understanding of the "heads down" directive. His solution seemed to serve both needs.

Figure 2.1   Double-Entry Notebook for Observations

Afterward, I used the notebook's right side to "conduct that 'continuing audit of meaning'" (Berthoff 1981, p. 45) that helped me understand my observations. The double-entry notebook gave me the opportunity to record and interpret information, as well as ask reflective questions, which I offer to help you begin an inquiry of your school's culture:

> What seems to be going on here?
> What are different perspectives from which this interaction can be viewed?
> What do students and adults seem to know about themselves and their role in this setting in order to get along and get things done?
> What seems to be most important to them in this situation?
> What connections can I make to other observations?
> What else do I need to know to better understand this situation?

Are You a Secretary or What?

The initial stage of rapport-building with fourth- and fifth-grade students took five months. I had not been in the building on a regular basis for two years and knew that I faced a challenge those first few weeks in September when I saw how difficult it was to make eye contact with most children when I passed them in the corridors and observed them in the cafeteria or on the playground. Campus school students see unfamiliar faces every day and learn to ignore them. They would get to know me if they needed to. That was how it worked in this school's culture. To their way of thinking, I could be a professor, older student teacher, or another lost college student looking for my class in the wrong wing.

After several weeks of cafeteria, corridor, playground, and classroom visibility, some students came to know me as the wife of fifth-grade teacher John Grayson (even though many demanded verification because I use a different surname from his). To others, I was their parents' junior high English teacher; still others recognized me as the supervisor with the clipboard who observed their student teacher during science, math, or reading lessons; some knew me as the "college teacher" who talked with their teacher about the methods students who read and wrote with them during their language arts time. A few students had trouble placing me at all. On the playground as I scribbled field notes, a fourth-grade boy stopped in mid-chase and asked, "Are you a secretary or what?" I told him, "No, I'm not. I'm here because I want to get to know you a bit before coming to your classroom to work with you."

A New Role

It is important to think about how your role is being perceived from the students' point of view. If a peer mediation program is to become accepted as part of a school's culture, consider the meaning of your involvement at this pre-program stage. In October 1992, I met with Clare Riley, the guidance counselor, and her intern Shari Rabinowitz; we made plans to team teach a series of forty-five-minute conflict resolution lessons to the ten classes of students who had first and second lunch and recess together—the times I planned to have peer mediators go on duty. When Clare Riley introduced me to each class, I took time to explain that we would be learning about conflict resolution for several months and that it would help me to start up a new program in January that was related to managing conflicts.

It might be useful to reflect on answers to these questions before you become involved in a peer mediation program in your school:

> What is my primary role in the school?
>
> What other roles have I had in the past?
>
> How do these roles connect to the one I will assume once the peer mediation program is introduced?

Building a Bridge

Introducing a curriculum that teaches conflict resolution skills to students seemed to be a sensible prelude to beginning a peer mediation program. I assumed that students who had even limited experience with conflict resolution activities would be able to step inside the mediation process, if they agreed to bring their conflict to peer mediators. I read Morton Deutsch's Executive Summary of an urban high school study, which painted a positive picture of his efforts:

> As students improved in managing their own conflicts (whether due to the training in conflict resolution and/or cooperative learning), they experienced increased social support and less victimization from others. This improvement in their relations with others led to increased self-esteem as well as a decrease in feelings of anxiety and depression and more frequent positive feelings of well-being. The higher self-esteem, in turn, produced a greater sense of personal control over their own fates. The increases in their sense of personal control and in their positive feelings of well-being led to higher academic performances. There is also indirect evidence that the work readiness and work performance of students were improved by their exposure to the training. Our data, further, indicate that "consumer satisfaction" with the training and its results were quite favorable— the students, teachers and administrators had generally positive views. (1993, p. 2)

There seems to be very little to dislike about this report. Positive results emanated from training administrators, coordinators, teachers, and paraprofessionals from three high schools in conflict resolution and/or cooperative learning theory and practices. Over a period of two years, Deutsch and his International Center for Cooperation and Conflict Resolution staff administered questionnaires and conducted interviews to gather data, making "systematic observations . . . of the training sessions, a random sample of students as they followed their daily schedules, and of various classroom and non-classroom activities" (p. 8). Theirs was an effort based on the entire staffs of three schools making a commitment to apply what they learned in the training to their interactions with students.

I had read program evaluations and research results offering evidence that students could be taught nonviolent strategies for settling disputes using principles of cooperation, negotiation, and conflict resolution and that students could become better equipped to deal with conflict in school, thereby helping to improve school climate (Benenson 1988; Stuart 1991; Davis and Porter 1985a;

Vermillion 1989; Welch 1989; Lane and McWhirter 1992; Satchel 1992; Ellsworth 1993). But I wondered if Hampton's students would acquire a peacemaker's Discourse from forty-five minutes of instruction every other week.

I believe that a conflict resolution curriculum can and should be used as a bridge to starting a peer mediation program and a method of maintaining it, but this brings a major issue to the forefront: the level of commitment and preparation among teachers and administrators. What happens if there is not the school-wide involvement and commitment that Deutsch's optimal combination of co-operative learning methods and a conflict resolution framework throughout the school day suggests?

I know from experience that there is a difference between a "bought" and "taught" curriculum. Many publishers now offer materials to support a conflict resolution curriculum. They are responding to a trend that begins with the hope that teaching students how to use language to navigate the conflict highway is more desirable than accepting escalating violence in schools. Hampton's secretaries feed faculty and staff mailboxes daily with a smorgasbord of curriculum catalogs.

Effective conflict resolution skills and strategies are not necessarily being learned and used by students simply because classroom teachers, guidance counselors, and health coordinators purchase materials. One story helps me to make a point few teachers would dispute.

A few years ago, I was having a casual discussion with a woman in my aerobics class who teaches at an urban public elementary school about twenty-five miles away from Riverton. When she asked me what topic I was thinking about for my dissertation, I mentioned conflict resolution and peer mediation. Her quick response was, "Oh, I know about that—we were given that big, white curriculum to do [Sadalla, Holmberg, and Halligan 1990]. It's still on my desk. I haven't had time to look at it yet." I was so struck by this brief exchange that I wrote it in my field notes when I arrived home. It seemed rich in implications and begged for a closer look. My friend seemed to believe that she "knew" about both topics. She seemed confident that knowledge could be accessed through a textbook: "Just give me the book and I'll teach what's in it." Another issue is embedded in her next words, "we were given." Classroom teachers are regularly plied with "new" curricula handed down from central administrative offices. I am one teacher who cannot recall ever being notified that any program be deleted from the wide range of lessons crammed into an already overflowing school day. "To do"—curricula are for doing without the necessary first steps of investigating a belief system that includes empowerment, self-determination, voluntariness, trust building, confidentiality, and neutrality. "It's still on my desk. I haven't had time to look at it yet." And when she does, its three-ring binder packaging invites her to pop out an activity for instant use.

My analysis should not be taken as a criticism of the teacher or any curriculum, but as a caution. A conflict resolution curriculum is aimed at improving students' problem-solving skills. An experiential curriculum, such as Sadalla, Holmberg, and Halligan's (1990) or Johnson and Johnson's (1991) or Kreidler's (1990) will give students experience in practicing these skills and strategies. But it is necessary to have committed, prepared, and informed adults invested in translating its powerful messages to students.

There is another more powerful interdependency necessary. Even if a core group of committed, trained mediators (teachers, administrators, parents, community program mediators) implement a peer mediation program, its success will still depend on classroom teachers providing all students with experiences in cooperative learning, conflict resolution, and negotiation skills (Johnson and Johnson 1991; Kreidler 1990). Brainstorming and other cooperative learning strategies must be woven throughout the fabric of content found in all curricular areas, such as Shatles' (1992) *Conflict Resolution Through Children's Literature: Impact II.*

M. A. Ellsworth (1993) looked at how a peer mediation program took hold in one middle school's culture. She stated,

> It is impossible under the most favorable conditions to bring a comprehensive change to a school if all staff cannot be trained and given the opportunity to reflect on how conflict resolution is or is not a part of their personal philosophies and education. The result is that a program that goes to the heart of one's everyday interactions may instead be incorporated partially at first as an add-on or new buzz words and catch phrases. It becomes objectified as a notebook full of lessons, a curriculum package. (p. 199)

After purchasing and reviewing several sets of materials from the National Association for Mediation in Education (Appendix A.6), Clare and I decided to use *Conflict Resolution: An Elementary School Curriculum* by Gail Sadalla, Meg Holmberg, and Jim Halligan (1990) because of its close relationship to her original scope and sequence and its emphasis on experiential learning. The white three-ring binder that holds the curriculum is arranged in two parts: the first section comprises a six-chapter, seemingly all-inclusive conflict resolution curriculum with over eighty activities that are labeled according to grade levels (K–1, 2–6, 4–6, K–6) and coded according to key and supplementary activities; the second section "describes how the skills learned through the Curriculum can be applied in the day-to-day life of the classroom and the school" (Intro–2).

I continued to establish the participant-observer role that would bring students, teachers, staff, and me into line with the peer mediation project I hoped to begin four months later. During the regularly scheduled biweekly guidance activity periods in October, November, and December, Clare, Shari, and I selected key activities designed to give students experiences in

- identifying conflict situations;
- appreciating individual points of view and cultural differences;
- developing a vocabulary for recognizing and describing feelings;
- using active listening to solve problems cooperatively.

By involving students in the activities, I hoped to learn what they knew about conflicts. I could also observe ways in which students related to partners or small groups. It is important to point out that conflict resolution was not being adopted as a schoolwide curriculum. So, Clare and I met with third-, fourth-, and fifth-grade teacher teams to share information about the lessons we planned for upcoming guidance activity periods. The teachers agreed to remain in the room while we taught the lessons.

She Took My Answer

"Let's brainstorm a list of words that come to mind when we think of the word *conflict*." We began our first lesson by going over the ground rules for brainstorming (Sadalla, Holmberg, and Halligan 1990, pp. 1–7):

1. Offer every idea that you can think of.
2. Do not criticize any idea—your own or anyone else's.
3. Think of as many ideas as possible within the time limit given.

I planned to connect these experiences with brainstorming when I introduced the mediation process to the same students months later. Two premises drive this crucial part of the process: Two or more heads are better than one; out of a seemingly "off the wall" solution could come a valid resolution.

Brainstorming during mediation works best if there has been experience with cooperative problem solving and the convergent and divergent thinking it fosters. It is at the later evaluating stage that disputants revise or rule out solutions in order to reach a fair and balanced agreement.

Each class's list of conflict words was impressive. Students were able to sort their words into positive, negative, or neutral categories and noticed the preponderance of negative perceptions of conflict ("pain," "fear," "violence," "screaming"). We discussed positive outcomes of conflict ("A problem could get solved." "You could be friends again.").

I wrote in my field notes about different reactions to the brainstorming activity. In some classrooms, it seemed as if students perceived that we wanted one correct answer, and readily competed for the chance to say it first, as opposed to understanding that we aimed to assemble a list cooperatively to show what we knew as a group about identifying conflicts. Each time one of us called on a student, others joined in with the lament, "She [or he] took *my* answer." Even when students did not verbalize this, there were disappointed looks or moans. It prompted me to say, "When you hear someone who gets called on give an answer that you would have given, you should feel good that you are on common ground with that person. Try to ask yourself: Good, now how can I build on that idea?"

In other classrooms, I noticed that the positive interdependence I had touched on above was already a feature of their classroom culture. Students skilled in communicating in a style supported by active listening would restate key ideas someone had just shared and say, "I'd like to piggyback on Joan's idea about bullying on the playground by adding . . ." "When Joan talked about bullying on the playground, it made me think about . . ." Students had acquired a language of response that their classroom teachers had taught them and that complemented the language of conflict resolution. Several teachers were taking a graduate course called "The Responsive Classroom," and their key text was Ruth Sidney Charney's (1991) *Teaching Children to Care: Management in the Responsive Classroom*. They were incorporating theory and practice into their daily routines.

Visiting ten classrooms on a regular basis gave me the opportunity to read another piece of classroom culture—seating arrangements. No two rooms were alike, but some shared certain features that reflected the teacher's belief in learning as being either socially or individually constructed. Students sat in clusters, U-shaped configurations, or rows. One teacher had moved the desks into different arrangements every time we arrived in what seemed like a frantic effort to control the hostile attitudes we saw his students frequently display. Our need to divide students into groups to work on the conflict resolution activities produced a dilemma. Do we have them count off and put all ones together, twos, and so on? Do we have students choose their own group? Do we work by table or sets of desks? In some classrooms, students seemed to be able to work with anyone. In others, I read body language that said, "I'm not working with her/him." There were times when students said it outright. Occasionally, a student would begin to cry when groups were formed. Since mediation is voluntary, I wondered if some students would be able to sit beside someone with whom they were having a dispute and construct a mutually satisfactory agreement.

Learning Experiences

Look for ways to understand students' experiences with cooperative or competitive learning. Observe how students respond to each other when working in pairs or small groups.

Prior to beginning a peer mediation program, invite teachers to share their beliefs about and experiences with cooperative learning (Deutsch 1982; Johnson and Johnson 1986) and learning theory and practice (Flood et al. 1991). Discuss these issues:

> What cooperative learning experiences do students have throughout the day?
> What competitive learning experiences do students have throughout the day?
> What conflict resolution curriculum and practices are being used in your school?

Not to Make You Feel Bad or Anything, But . . .

Clare and I were in the midst of presenting a "You-Message/I-Message Skit" (Sadalla, Holmberg, and Halligan 1990, pp. 4–19) in which one girl's accusation of gossip is met with insults and name-calling. We delivered version B, the I-Message, with appropriate shifts in our tone of voice (angry to sincere), eye contact (fiery to calm), and body language (menacing to relaxed):

> *Marie:* I was really angry when I heard that you told people I was going to fight Darlene after school. We had already made up, and she got angry all over again. I was also hurt that what I told you in private as a friend, you told to other people. I want to be your friend, but I feel like I can't trust you right now. I need to know that anything I tell you will be kept between us.
>
> *Anita:* I'm sorry, Marie. I feel really bad about messing things up because I really like you, and I was only trying to help. I don't want to lose you as a friend, and I promise I won't do anything like that again. If you

ever tell me anything in private, I will keep it to myself. If you want, we could go talk to Darlene together, and I'll tell the other kids that you two have settled everything.

Fifth-grade student Terry Cortez raised his hand and said, "Not to make you feel bad or anything, but the second one is the way they talk on television." Students come to school equipped with lessons learned at home, their primary Discourse community, and the neighborhood, which is one of many secondary Discourse communities to which they will belong (Gee 1990, pp. 149–54). The language of conflict resolution may either be harmonious or dissonant to students' ears. Terry's reading of "I-message" language was that it was not what he heard in his primary or secondary Discourse communities. He recognized mismatches among his home, neighborhood, and school Discourses.

"True," I said, "it's a different way of talking, Terry. Your choice of television characters is interesting because some people believe that we play lots of roles every day and make decisions about how we're going to talk and act, depending on where we are and who we are with." I drew a diagram with "Terry" in the center and asked, "Let's think about some of the different roles you might play each day. Let's start with one you are in right now." I wrote "student." "Are there some others?" By the time we finished, Terry acknowledged several Discourse identities: son, nephew, soccer player, friend, churchgoer. "Terry, do you talk and act exactly the same way when you are with people who expect you to be 'in your role'?" He scanned his memory. "No, because the way I talk with my friends is *way different* from how I talk with my aunt." A chuckle of recognition bounced around the room.

"During these weeks, we are trying to introduce you to a way of using language when you're having a conflict that might be different from what you are used to now. Like anything we teach you in school, it's up to you to decide when and where to use it, or if you're going to use it at all."

During an interview, Terry pinpointed another mismatch between conflict resolution Discourse and his own that occurred during active listening when the listener restates the speaker's key ideas in order to determine whether or not he or she has been understood correctly. Recommended bridges between listening and restating are: "What I heard you say is . . ." and "Let me see if understood what you just said . . ." Terry said, "I have a problem with [restating] because I don't think there's any reason for it. 'Cause I think they should hear it right the first time."

Terry seemed to believe that one's ability to listen "actively" meant you listened so well that restating was unnecessary and, in fact, would have a negative effect on the speaker, causing him or her to "have a problem." Instead of increasing his capacity to participate more fully in this social interaction, restating diminished it. This was an effect opposite from the one intended in conflict resolution Discourse, which does not assume everyone is a skilled listener or that everyone comes from a lifetime of experiences of being heard. Terry's analysis made me realize that "local meanings" (Erickson 1982, p. 167) could grow up around the practice of restating and might have an impact on students' acceptance of mediation process, which relies heavily on restating.

Mismatches

It is important to be alert to students' verbal and nonverbal expressions of mismatches between in-school conflict resolution styles and alternatives being offered to them through your planned curriculum. Observe and interview students in order to understand their perceptions about these likenesses and differences.

Following are some issues you might discuss with students:

What does it mean to have a conflict? a fight?

What are some kinds of conflicts or fights that are likely in school?

What are some ways students settle conflicts in school?

How are conflict resolution methods different from ways students would usually solve conflicts?

He Took My Seat

During the weeks prior to beginning the peer mediation program, one of the routines I regularly observed was lunchtime. Sparks of students' animated conversations illuminated significant moments as I circulated among tables where they sat grouped by classrooms. As I passed one table, I overheard an Anglo-American boy chanting, "You got cooties" over and over, just loud enough for the Asian-American boy fuming silently across from him to hear. This interaction lasted less than a minute before the teaser decided to stop and resume eating.

In those early days of observing in the cafeteria, students would often mistake me for a duty teacher and ask if they could return their empty trays or use the bathroom. I would point out a teacher and say, "You need to ask ———."

A small third-grade Asian-American boy walked over to me and said, "He took my seat." He lifted his lunch tray in the direction of a bigger Anglo-American boy at the end of a table nearby. I recognized the pair—he was the same child who had endured the cootie chant days before, and his opponent was the same boy.

"What can you do about it?" I asked.

His puzzled expression showed me that he was doing what he was supposed to be doing about this problem. Didn't I understand that?

"You need to see Mrs. Beauchamp, then." I watched as he walked over to the teacher and repeated the story of his plight. She marched over to the squatter and said firmly, "Move." He did and the conflict ended. Or did it?

This vignette shows that the victim's overt social behavior fit in with the adult established standard or norm of not losing one's temper and seeking an adult to intervene in a conflict situation. He chose silence in the face of his tormenter's teasing. He could have reached over and hit him or called him a name. Other students reacted in these ways. But he might find himself in Mr. Reynolds' office, and that could mean more trouble.

The signal to depend on adults to resolve conflicts was being sent to students in Hampton's culture. I observed a teacher praising a student for doing "the right thing" when, instead of handling it himself, he complained to the teacher that another boy had cut in front of him in the lunch line.

In each case, underlying issues between the two boys were not examined or resolved. What makes someone tease another? Why take someone else's seat? Why move to someone else's place in line? Encouraging students to resolve conflicts by simply turning to adults for immediate justice seems like correcting surface errors in a student's composition with a red pen: it takes care of obvious, but not underlying, needs of the disputants.

Another day, I sat at an empty table in the lunchroom and watched the third- and fourth-grade students line up for outdoor recess. A dark-haired Hispanic boy left his table and plunked down opposite me.

"Are you going to recess?" I asked.

"No," he said flatly. Then, "I hate this school."

"Oh?"

"Yeah, you get beat up here, and they leave you on the ground. I want to go back to my old school."

"Where's that?"

He named one of the other five elementary schools in Riverton. "Reinhart."

"What happens there when you get beat up?"

"They get suspended."

"What happens here?"

"They throw you on the ground and leave you there. You should have seen this morning. Three people were fighting before school. They were kicking and punching someone on the ground."

"What happened to the students who were beating the person up?"

"Nothing."

It seemed as though this student's understanding of justice and his perception of safety did not match Hampton's pro-social system, in which students sometimes paid their consequences through in-house suspensions. But to this new student, no out-of-school suspension meant no consequences.

Some students viewed Hampton's discipline structure differently from Jim Reynolds, who shared his (adult) point of view on the effect of his sending the discipline report home in Chapter 1. Students Kristi Tesadore, Billy Glenn, Elizabeth Garrett, and T. J. Jackson described how they saw conflicts resolved at Hampton:

> *Elizabeth:* Mr. Reynolds sits there at his computer and writes it up.
>
> *T. J.:* Yeah. And the next day, you're going to be even madder at that kid.
>
> *Billy:* Some kids try to beat that letter home and say [assumes sweet child's voice], "I'll get the mail" and then shove it under their porch.
>
> *Kristi:* I'm not criticizing Mr. Reynolds, but when you go to his office, you don't really solve the problem. People keep going back there and going back there, and going back there . . .

In fact, Jim Reynolds verified Kristi's perception by developing a data base showing that 67 percent of the disciplinary incidents he handled over a three-month period involved the same fourteen students. It was a phenomenon also noted by Satchel (1992) in a study on increasing pro-social behavior of elementary students through a conflict resolution program.

Patterns

As you review and analyze existing conflict resolution procedures in your school, try to recognize at what point a third party may intervene. Identify consequences and look for patterns.

Apply the following questions to your findings:

What role do adults play in resolving students' conflicts?
How do students seem to perceive their ability to resolve conflicts without adult intervention?
How do adults seem to perceive students' ability to resolve their own conflicts?

Let Me Help!

I found that another aspect of a school's culture merited attention before I implemented a peer mediation program: students' perceptions of themselves as contributing members of the school's community.

My memories of being a first-year teacher in 1964 include sitting at my desk, cutting out construction-paper hands to staple to the bulletin board that was to become a permanent feature of my third-grade classroom. These were the Helping Hands that had students' names pinned to them during our Monday-morning ritual of choosing helpers. "Pick me!" "Let me help!" Trios and quartets of voices and hands rose and fell as the parade of job opportunities marched by. I came to accept the inevitable disappointed sighs, and was impressed even then by the hierarchy of prestige that accompanied this activity. The most sought-after positions took them out of the classroom—taking the attendance to the office or picking up milk from the cafeteria for our morning snack. Most jobs were based in the classroom—watering plants, sharpening pencils, or passing out paper. I remember keeping a separate roster of names in order to keep track of who had which jobs, so that I wouldn't hear, "She did that before."

When I began teaching, I believed that it benefitted students to become responsible members of our classroom community. I thought students' helping to maintain the classroom was like eating Wonder Bread for one's character. Today I know more about nutrition and more about students. I realize that they need the multi-grain bread that broader involvement in the school would provide to nourish their sense of community.

I needed to understand that

> it all starts with a school admitting the school is a community. Strangers don't mediate. It is in the interest of an on-going relationship that motivates people to resolve a dispute . . . Ethics deals with conduct, with ways we treat others. Schools with mediation programs are schools that recognize that they are communities. (Dreyfuss 1990, p. 26)

Thirty years ago, I assumed that doling out classroom responsibilities would build students' self-esteem ("I am thought of as capable and trustworthy") and a sense of community ("If I do my job well, others will benefit"). I was assuming that my third-grade students' sense of responsibility would not only sustain them through our ten months together, but spill over into the rest of their lives. I ignored the larger community outside my classroom. My view of community was painfully narrow, considering what I have learned over the past three years as peer mediation coordinator/trainer.

Helpers

In addition to participating in academic subjects, what can students do to become involved in their school's community? The following suggestions may assist you in identifying helping roles available to students at the schoolwide level:

- List after-school and extra curricular programs.
- Analyze them according to activities that place students in helping roles.
- Consider program goals, benefits, and rewards or recognition that are connected to them.
- Explore selection processes by asking which students have access to these roles and how participants are perceived by others in the school.

If I placed a time-lapse camera in the corridors, offices, library, and cafeteria of Hampton Campus School, you would see spurts of activity amid quiet, deserted times. Students from several primary and intermediate classrooms travel back and forth once each week to keep their book-buddy commitments. A team of fifth-grade students moves through the school each morning to distribute the attendance and office announcements. John Grayson has trained a group of fifth-grade volunteers from his class to be computer technicians; they arrive twenty minutes before school and get the lab up and running for the rest of the school.

Before beginning the peer mediation program, I asked Donna Dignon, Hampton's bookkeeper/secretary, to describe some of the reasons that students come into the office.

"They might have been injured on the playground at recess, or they might have gotten into a fight before school, or they might have just gotten really wet on the way to school playing in puddles. They might have been fresh on the bus and have to see the assistant principal to be kicked off the bus . . . If anyone picked on them, they'll come in.

"Then there are other children who come in just to drop off attendance that we see in that way. They haven't done anything wrong. They're just here to do a little errand."

"So they're helpers?"

"We do have a little volunteer program where students can come in and do community service and get a prize at the end of the year for how many hours they put in. They do copying, collating, stapling, cleaning the windowsills, dusting the file cabinets, stacking or sorting paper. We teach them how we want it and they stack it and deliver it. They've been wonderful. They help us a lot."

"If I were a kid, how would I get to volunteer?"

"You would probably be a fourth- or fifth-grader who would approach your teacher. We've informed teachers about this program. When we have work to be done, we call the teachers and tell them and they call back and say, 'Well, I can send you two now or at recess, if they want to volunteer.'"

Donna described the sign-in book and prize and ice cream reward system at the end of the year. She chuckled as she said, "And they don't let you forget that they volunteered."

"What have you noticed about children who do volunteer service?"

"There were a few, maybe three, kids that would fight and get into trouble outside, but they do wonderful work when they're volunteering. So it's amazing that they do both. They get into little scuffles and when they're getting punished, they can't help us. They'll sit right in our office and they know that we need things done and say to us, 'Oh, can I help out while I'm sitting here?' But that would be almost like a reward. They love doing those little jobs, so we tell them, 'No, the days you don't get in trouble, you can help out.'"

I thought about how eagerly my students vied for the job of bringing the attendance to the office and how it was perceived by Donna as a "little errand" because the attendance was only one of the office's many paper-driven functions. The office volunteer program was abandoned a year later when a new principal was appointed. But when it was a part of Hampton's culture, office work seemed to be perceived as a reward. Only well-behaved students need volunteer.

Donna noticed that some students would do "wonderful work when they're volunteering" and yet still "get into trouble." She thought it "amazing" that they managed seemingly contradictory roles—volunteer and troublemaker. A perception like this was significant because I knew it would resonate throughout the peer mediator selection process to take place in the coming months. Negative leaders—students who regularly responded to conflict in inappropriate ways—would be a necessary component of the group of volunteer mediators (Sadalla, Holmberg, and Halligan 1990, pp. II–12). I wondered how Hampton's students and adults would react to the idea of Hampton's negative leaders as peer mediators.

As you observe in your school and interview adults and students about available helping roles, keep these questions in mind:

> What categories would helping roles sort into: clerical, teaching, maintenance, problem solving?
> Do students volunteer or are they selected?
> Which students have access to helping roles?
> Do age, gender, behavior, or scholastic standing factors affect students' access to helping roles?
> Where are students perceived as being "in place" and "out of place" in school?
> What helping roles take students outside classrooms? outside school?
> When and where can students go unattended by adults?
> How do students seem to see themselves and others in helping roles?

Consider Davis and Porter's "Ten Reasons for Instituting a School-Based Mediation Program" (Figure 2.2). Notice that they are written from an adult's perspective and imply serious and important work will be necessary in order to implement a peer mediation program. Look at your observation notes and ask yourself: Do students in my school seem to be perceived by adults as capable, caring people? What opportunities do they have to practice an ethic of social responsibility? Is the climate in my school conducive to students' taking on a new helping role?

Nel Noddings (1984) urged educators to give students opportunities to be "contributing" persons (p. 65). She stated that "the child in the process of build-

---

Ten Reasons for Instituting a School-Based Mediation Program

A review of program descriptions reveals that the following reasons most commonly motivate those who wish to promote mediation in the schools.

1. Conflict is a natural human state often accompanying changes in our institutions or personal growth. It is better approached with skills than avoidance.
2. More appropriate and effective systems are needed to deal with conflict in the school setting than expulsion, suspension, court intervention, and detention.
3. The use of mediation to resolve school-based disputes can result in improved communication between and among students, teachers, administrators, and parents and can, in general, improve the school climate as well as provide a forum for addressing common concerns.
4. The use of mediation as a conflict resolution method can result in a reduction of violence, vandalism, chronic school absence, and suspension.
5. Mediation training helps both young people and teachers to deepen their understanding about themselves and others and provides them with lifetime dispute resolution skills.
6. Mediation training increases students' interest in conflict resolution, justice, and the American legal system while encouraging a higher level of citizenship activity.
7. Shifting the responsibility for solving appropriate school conflicts from adults to young adults and children frees both teachers and administrators to concentrate more on teaching than on discipline.
8. Recognizing that young people are competent to participate in the resolution of their own disputes encourages student growth and gives students skills—such as listening, critical thinking, and problem solving—that are basic to all learning.
9. Mediation training, with its emphasis upon listening to others' points of view and the peaceful resolution of differences, assists in preparing students to live in a multicultural world.
10. Mediation provides a system of problem solving that is uniquely suited to the personal nature of young people's problems and is frequently used by students for problems they would not take to parents, teachers, or principals.

Figure 2.2   Ten Reasons for Instituting a School-Based Mediation Program. (*Albie Davis and Kit Porter, "Tales of Schoolyard Mediation,"* Update on Law-Related Education, *Winter 1985, Volume 9, p. 27. Reprinted with permission of Albie Davis and Kit Porter.*)

ing an ethical ideal needs practice in caring. Simply talking about or writing about caring is a poor substitute for actual caring" (p. 122). During these past three years, I learned that Hampton students wanted the opportunity to do serious, caring work, and they wanted to be taken seriously when they did it.

A Step Back to Reflect

Taking time to observe students using the "tools of culture" to understand and resolve conflicts in their school before implementing a peer mediation program is an investment that could affect its success.

> Dreyfuss (1990) criticized traditional disciplinary procedures because they are
>
> unimaginative, noncreative, and stifling. Discipline policies fail to prepare students to live in a democratic society or in an unsupervised world . . . The critical flaw in school discipline is its emphasis on punishment. It thwarts the development of student responsibility, leadership, independence, and interdependence. It works against the stated curriculum objectives of critical thinking and problem solving . . . Students are told that natural consequences will flow from their act. But justice is often delayed and fact finding is flawed. School discipline fails to be convincingly fair, impartial, or supportive of human dignity. (p. 22)

As I began formulating plans for Hampton's peer mediation program, I felt confident that its disciplinary system did not fit into the traditional patterns that Dreyfuss described in her article, "Learning Ethics in School-Based Mediation Programs." A description of the "pro-social approach" that was included in the cover letter accompanying the assistant principal's Pro-Social Action Report helped me begin to understand what Hampton's students were experiencing *from an adult's point of view* (see Chapter 1).

In my quest to discover ways in which the system of conflict resolution works in the school's culture, I had several talks with Jim Reynolds. During an interview prior to beginning the peer mediation program, I told him that I noticed a similarity between the cooperative problem-solving language of Hampton's pro-social approach ("all the parties get together to discuss the situation, the problem, and the solution and to determine the consequence") and the peer mediation process. Reynolds agreed and described how, in addition to the pro-social approach that he used, adult mediators from the community mediation program had come into the school during the 1991–92 school year "probably six or seven times" to settle disputes. His involvement was minimal: "We [he and the principal] wouldn't have any part in it. The mediator would show up, both kids, both parents, and they'd go off to the room that we found for them, and the only thing I would get is the agreement."

I remember being glad that the term "mediation" might not be completely unknown to students, but Jim Reynolds' final statement alerted me to the fact that I would need to think about who would receive copies of an agreement made by nine- and ten-year-old children. I knew that this is a sensitive and complex issue that has implications for everyone involved because it affects confidentiality and trust. Throughout these early months, I gathered all the information I could about the existing system of conflict resolution at Hampton and continued asking myself, "Whose point of view does this piece represent?" "How will it support or conflict with a peer mediation program?"

CHAPTER THREE

≈ ≈

Understand Your Community's Culture

I Never Go Out at Night

Hampton Campus School's district is unique and ordinary. It is ordinary because it has a neighborhood school that draws its 547 students from a small, industrial, urban population of approximately 41,000. It is unique because of the school's location on the campus of a state college. It is ordinary because residents and workers experience their fair share of conflicts as spectators or participants. It is unique because the school district's widely diverse population of blue- and white-collar workers, college students, and welfare families could be viewed as a microcosm of the larger American society. A brisk five-minute walk south of the campus would place you on streets where the homeless loiter, and drug dealers and prostitutes proffer their goods and services. A five-minute walk north would take you to roads where middle- and upper-income, single-family homes are protected by security systems and watchdogs. I have noticed similar extremes in socioeconomic strata played out vertically in mid-town Manhattan, where skyscrapers lift the well-to-do up and away from the grinding poverty and crime below. In Riverton, these conditions are laid out horizontally along a few dozen streets (Figure 3.1).

A front-page article in the *Riverton Gazette* featured the latest round of violence on the streets abutting the south side of Riverton State's campus. A twenty-year-old Hispanic man from Lincoln, a city that borders Riverton, was visiting friends on Grant Street. As they all stood on the sidewalk, a short, heavily built African-American man appeared and randomly shot at the group with his 9mm semiautomatic weapon, hitting the Lincoln man in the thigh. The shooter turned, walked away, and could not be found by police.

The police captain was amazed that more people were not struck by any of the eleven rounds that had been fired. The reporter interviewed several neighbors, who said that the shooting was probably linked to drug trafficking. Residents went on to describe the brazen attitude of dealers who sell drugs, loiter, fight, and set fires.

David and Hannah Weston told the reporter that they had been living on Grant Street for twenty-eight years, but that the violence was getting worse. Mrs. Weston "saw about thirty people on the street before the gunshots," which left her three grandsons, ages eight, ten, and eleven "unable to sleep the rest of the night."

Mr. and Mrs. Weston are the grandparents and guardians of Jason Militades,

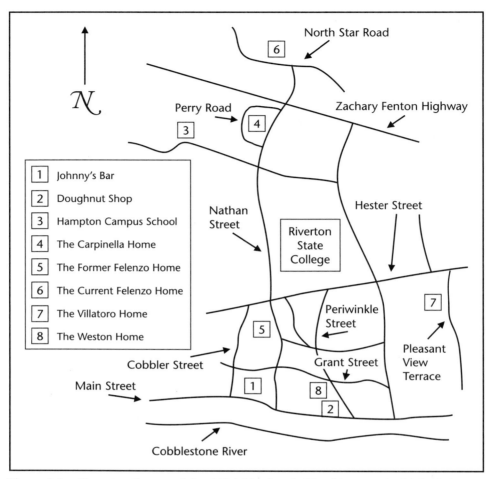

Figure 3.1 Hampton Campus School Neighborhood. *(Graphic representation by JoAnn Pellecchia.)*

a soft-spoken fifth-grade student with short blond hair and blue eyes. Hampton students looked up to Jason because he excelled in sports, making his own headlines on the local sports pages as an outstanding soccer player.

When the article appeared in the newspaper, I asked him if he would let me interview him about it—with his grandparents' approval—and tell me what it was like to live on Grant Street. He brought a signed release letter from home the next day. We sat in my office where I had several newspaper clippings about his neighborhood on the table. As we talked, Jason's eyes swept the floor as if he were retrieving experiences from memory using his special vantage point from above:

> We live on the third floor, and my aunt, uncle, and cousin live on the first floor. My aunt is in the most danger because they live so close to the street. She is going to have a baby any day now.

Whenever I hear hollering or a big bang outside, I crawl to my brother's bedroom window at the front of the house and peek between the blinds. [He made slits with his fingers and peeked out between them to show me.]

One night, I heard people fighting on the sidewalk and looked out. A woman was hitting a guy with a big, black stick screaming, "Get off my boyfriend" because the guy was choking him while he held him across the hood of a car.

Another time, I saw a guy on the sidewalk get in a fight, and they broke his nose. The next time I saw him from the window, he had it all taped up. These people are from the Fruit Belt [the other section of Riverton noted for drug trafficking and violence], Lincoln, and New York City. They come here to deal drugs. Once, when my younger brother and I were walking home, there were some people on the sidewalk and when we walked by them, one held out a white bag [crack cocaine] in front of us. We kept on walking.

Jason searched through the pile of articles, located a September 7 newspaper story about a stabbing and said, "I came home from school that day, and there was a long red stripe [of blood] on the sidewalk. I only play in my backyard, and I never go out at night."

Understanding conflicts, including those Jason viewed from his third-floor perch, begins with recognizing that all conflict is tangled in a web of three basic causes (Figure 3.2). Conflict occurs when people perceive threats or imbalances to

psychological and physical needs (self respect, respect from others, safety, shelter, clothing, food);

resources (money, housing, land, students, funding);

culturally learned beliefs and values (religious, ethnic, class, race, gender).

Jason was experiencing conflict. Although the violent acts he described were not directed at him personally, his physical and psychological need for safety was being threatened, and he was powerless to act in his own defense. Notice how he was first concerned for his pregnant aunt. In a sadly perceptive way, he surmised that she was in the "most danger" because of her apartment on the first floor. He knew that bullets could pierce walls and shatter windows.

Hamachek (1988) suggested criteria for "evaluating self-concept and ego development" using Erikson's psychosocial framework. These criteria helped me understand the effect of growing up in an atmosphere of mistrust "in the sense of a readiness for danger and an anticipation of discomfort" (Erikson, quoted in Hamachek 1988, p. 355). Would it be difficult to understand why children like Jason might assume that "people are generally bad or evil" or that they could tend "to focus on the negative aspects of others' behavior" or might behave "in a relatively guarded and closed manner when around others" (p. 355)? Would it be difficult to understand why children growing up in a violent situation would use violent solutions to their conflicts in school? Would it be difficult to understand why they might have a difficult time volunteering to sit next to their opponents and trust them to mediate a dispute?

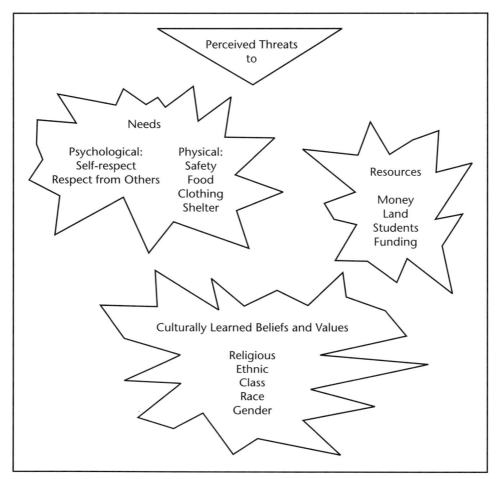

Figure 3.2 Sources of Conflict

Until fifth grade, Jason used physical violence to settle some of his disputes at school. I have the Pro-Social Action Reports to support what he readily admitted. The consequences were in-house suspensions. At home, Jason watched pulsing lights from police cruisers turn the night air blue while officers firmly inserted sidewalk idlers into the back seats of cruisers and into paddy wagons. However, more of the same stock characters took their places, and some of the original cast members returned. Jason saw broken noses bandaged, then healed. Life went on. If and when he chose to use violence to settle a dispute, it would be easy to assume that he was imitating a pattern that, even at this writing, he can witness from his brother's bedroom window—in spite of the Riverton police department's efforts to quell drug trafficking and prostitution.

Adults model behavior for children. Jason's story is testimony to the fact that children are watching, sometimes from hiding places, as adults are embroiled in conflicts. And their sophistication in analyzing what they are seeing can be startling.

Lea Rodriguez was a fourth-grade student who lived on Cobbler Street, one block from Jason. One day, we talked while she ate lunch. She mentioned her upcoming move to North Carolina.

"It will be better there." She nodded to emphasize the truth of her statement as she opened her lunch box to take out her fruit drink and salami sandwich. A pickle spear had leaked its juice and became the smell dominating our conversation.

"How will it be better?" I asked.

"Well, no shoot-outs like at the house in back [on Nathan Street]."

"Shoot-outs?"

"I look out my window. They shoot their guns." She held her small hand up and worked her finger into position to pull an imaginary trigger.

"Are they shooting at someone?"

"No." She was pointing her finger toward the ceiling. "Up in the air."

"Why do you think that they do that?"

She paused, and then said thoughtfully, "A tradition, I suppose."

Lea grew more animated with her next observation. "And when people call the police, when they come, guess what? No guns."

"Where are they?"

"In the trunk."

"In the trunk? How do you know?"

"I see them run down to their cars. When they come back upstairs, no more guns." At this Lea's blue-green eyes grew wide in mock innocence, and she opened her palm to show nothing. Lea, her brother, and mother moved to North Carolina a few weeks later.

A *tradition*. Astute analysis coming from a nine-year-old. Beyond the danger, beyond the lawlessness, I found it hard to challenge Lea's perception that what she was seeing was a kind of men's macho gunplay. Her worldview was one where violence was part of a tradition situated in an ever-widening vortex that gained energy whenever she turned on her television or picked up a newspaper.

In my quest to find out more about Hampton students' home and community environments, I asked parents from each of three economically diverse Hampton Campus School neighborhoods to describe what it was like to live there. My assumption in choosing a parent from each neighborhood (as well as one who had the special perspective of moving from the south side of campus to the north side) was that there might be a chance of interviewing at least one renter. However, all three were home owners in a city that, according to city records, was divided equally with respect to home owners and renters.

Ana Villatoro grew up in an apartment in Brooklyn and is aware of the violence around Cobbler Street, which is four blocks away from her home in Riverton. She and her husband, Saul, tried to sell their house for six of the eleven years they lived on Pleasant View Terrace, a street at the southeastern edge of Riverton State College's campus. Houses are close together and sit right on the street. Ana would have preferred a front lawn and bigger backyard for her three children to play. It would take about ten minutes to walk to Hampton, but she drove them each day. Ana used to work for a government research group, but left full-time employment to be home with her children.

> My kids play in the neighborhood. They have points to where they can
> go. To the corner and that's it. A lot of Hampton kids from up toward

Cobbler Street live in apartments. They feel like they're in the city. I don't want to let Ricky go alone with them.

The difference is that they are more independent and do things on their own. Those kids are more daring. Here, the neighbors all look out for each other. We're not nosy, but it is a little group here. If we say something to our kids, they listen. But, if it's a kid from up there, they'll tell you off.

I won't let Ricky go up there unless I know the parents. It's drugs and worse. One day, when I was driving my fourteen-year-old daughter to the high school, she asked, "Who's that woman there?" I said, "Wait a minute. That's too close to home. She working—so early in the morning, she's waiting to see who will pick her up." People don't realize that it's in our neighborhood.

Both Ana's and Jason's perceptions of his neighborhood were consistent with each other: being there posed threats to personal safety and affronts to values. Simmering conflicts could be dangerous to innocent bystanders. Added into Ana's way of looking at things was her assessment of the children living there: they were ready to "tell you off" if censured by adults. These were the same Hampton students who played kick ball at recess and sat next to her son, Ricky, in his classroom.

Invisibility. Concealment. Avoidance. Ana's "to the corner and that's it" rule and Jason's "I never go out at night" were echoed by Joan Carpinella, who grew up on Hester Street and lives with her husband and two children in what used to be her grandparents' house on Perry Road, north of Riverton State's campus. She highlighted her feelings of danger by saying,

My kids don't leave the immediate neighborhood that much. People say that all this recent violence is "not in my neighborhood," but it's pretty darned close because it's on the other side of the campus. There was a time when I'd go anywhere in this city. Now I don't go out at night or on the south side of campus alone. There was a time when I never locked my door when I was home, but now I do. We have a watchdog. I'm nervous, sad, and scared.

Ana's and Joan's singular point of view is supported by Laura Felenzo, who came to Riverton from a middle-class suburban community outside Boston in 1976. She has a long personal history in Riverton that began when she lived on campus as a college student, then in apartments around Jason's neighborhood. When she married a Riverton native whom she met during her senior year at the college, they bought a house on Cobbler Street. That was over ten years ago.

When I first interviewed Laura, she and her family had just moved into a custom-built home in a new development on North Star Road. At the time, three of her four children attended Hampton Campus School.

When my husband and I first bought our home on Cobbler Street, our biggest problem was trespassing by the college students. It slowly changed when some of the college students moved out [to newly constructed residence halls] and more single mothers moved in. It turned into Section 8 housing [for] welfare mothers.

First, it was Black[s], then Puerto Ricans and Asians. They all didn't get along. There was a Puerto Rican corner, a Black corner, and some Asians over there. If it was warm weather, it would start in the afternoon and go on until three, four, five in the morning. It was territorial: certain people would walk on certain sides of the street—it would be like an avoidance thing.

One time, I saw someone go by carrying a rifle. I was so naive that I thought it was a toy. The [neighborhood] kids told me it was real. When the shootings started all around us, my husband decided that we had enough. My kids were at Hampton by then, and we wanted to keep them there because we liked what was going on. We bought a piece of land up on North Star Road about three years ago, but didn't finish building our house and move in until three months ago.

The streets bordering the southern edge of Riverton State's campus were perceived as dangerous. In August 1995, a newspaper article quoted a college vice president who said that

surveys conducted by the college have shown that students remain fearful of the troubled neighborhood despite increased police patrols there. Although the college is near the center of town, he said, students are reluctant to walk through the neighborhood to reach the downtown. Instead, most students do their shopping on [Zachary Fenton] Highway.

When threats to safety occurred in Riverton, it seemed that the pattern of conflict resolution at work in each story was the same:

Try to move away.
Stay in hiding or close to home.
Call in the authorities (the police).

Needs

I believe that we need to understand and appreciate the presence of conflict in everyone's lives and know that children are observing how adults resolve problems. Each community reflects a social and economic history, contains ingredients that serve up special mixes of conflict, and develops systems for resolving or enduring them. Listening to each story, it was hard not to notice the feeling of isolation that emanated from the storytellers—Jason crouching at his brother's bedroom window; Ana mentioning the presence of her immediate neighbors "look[ing] out for each other." Missing from each is a sense of community, of belonging to, of being cared for by the larger community.

Weeks before Lea and I talked about her watching men participating in their gunplay ritual, she shared a more hopeful aspect of her life. When I interviewed her as one of the sixty-three students who volunteered to become Hampton's first peer mediators, she told about sitting under a tree in her backyard talking with her friends about their problems and trying to figure out ways to solve them. She referred to my classroom presentation [discussed in Chapter 5] and said, "[Mediation] reminds me of what we do under the tree." Lea was able to connect a peacemaking strategy that she practiced in her world with one she was learning about in school. Jason, who also volunteered to become a peer mediator, would at one point say that the experience had helped him to "give up fighting first and try to talk it out" when he had a conflict.

It is important to assess threats to the physical and psychological needs in your school's community because students bring their home and community conflict resolution lessons into school. If they are to learn other strategies to add to their repertoire, they will need to match the school's conflict resolution curriculum and peer mediation program with their home and neighborhood cultures.

The following questions will be central to an exploration of your school's community:

> What perceived threats to psychological and physical needs are present?
>
> With respect to psychological and physical needs, how does the wider community model conflict resolution when threats are posed?

They Rent

Ricky Villatoro was absent the day the art teacher worked with the peer mediators to silk-screen their symbol onto our blue tee shirts. I asked Ricky if he would stay after school to help screen his shirt and a few others. He agreed, so I called Ana and told her that I would drive Ricky home when we were done.

As he got out of my car, Ricky looked up at a man working on a roof across the street and said, "That's Allison's father." (She was another fourth-grade student.) I said, "Looks like he's fixing his roof." Ricky nodded, but found it necessary to add one more piece of information: "They rent."

Ricky's words lingered with me because I had not expected ownership to be an issue worthy of comment, especially from a ten-year-old. After rereading interview transcripts, newspaper clippings, and documents, two resource-based conflicts emerged involving two groups of owners: home owners like Ana and Laura, and Riverton State College.

While students are any college's main resource, their presence created certain tensions in Riverton's neighborhoods. Ricky's mother told me about noticing "a difference when the [college] kids come in because they make a lot of noise, and in the summer we have a peaceful time here [on Pleasant View Terrace] . . . When they come in, you hear screaming at midnight, and they're outside making noise. I've gone out and said, 'Could you keep it down? The kids are sleeping.' It gets rowdy." She saw a quagmire of responsibility: the neighbors blame the college students for "vandalism or screaming" so the problem is not their fault. When Ana described neighborhood conflicts, she said, "Whatever happens, they blame the area, but they don't blame themselves." Laura, who lived on Cobbler Street, described police coming to break up the parties, and party-goers throwing cases of beer over her stone wall and hiding in their fenced-in backyard until the police left. She added in disgust, "They would urinate all over the place."

The college administration's relationship with off-campus students and neighborhood residents presented a quandary: leaning too far into students' lives could hamper the college's ability to attract and keep students, thus threatening student enrollment, a key funding source. Enforcing off-campus behavior restrictions would be biting the proverbial hand that fed them. Still, the college needed to be perceived as a good neighbor and took steps to publicly acknowledge and address certain problems.

Riverton State College's President James Malone convened a Neighborhood Task Force to look at "the relationship of the college to the immediate neighborhood." The resulting report listed five issues that coincided with what parents implied or articulated to me:

1. There is a perception in the neighborhood that the college is largely apathetic about the city and its residents.
2. There is no broad-based and formal college/community link.
3. There is lack of formal college representation on important community committees.
4. There is no clearly identified point of contact for the community with the college.
5. Faculty and administrators who devote time and energy to the local community do not feel that their contributions are recognized as important to the college.

Recommendations included the establishment of an Office of Community Relations and the appointment of a racially and culturally diverse College-Community Advisory Committee to address issues identified by the task force. Another effort publicized in the regional newspaper cited an incentive program wherein "first-time home buyers in the college neighborhood will be eligible to receive tuition credits for evening classes at the school. Also, the college has agreed to give preference in hiring to neighborhood residents and will offer technical help to property owners who undertake renovations."

I began to understand this conflict when I viewed it from two points of view: the college's resource (students) was being threatened, while Ana's property value and quality of life in the neighborhood were being threatened by the college's resource (students). The college's efforts included forming a committee that would work to improve communication between itself and the neighborhood and "offering free tuition and other incentives to encourage home ownership and improvements in the crime-plagued college neighborhood."

An institution's need for space can be a source of conflict if it is situated in an urban neighborhood. Laura described a second resource-based conflict between home owners and the college:

> There is a piece of land between Cobbler and Nathan streets where a home was torn down. We approached [the college] and they refused to sell it to us. We didn't have a driveway, and we would have used it to park the cars.
>
> If we would have been smarter, we would have known that RSC didn't own it. They deceived us and made us think that they did own it because they had plans for it. If we had fenced it in, it would have been ours.

Eminent domain. When they saw that we were interested in it, they fenced it in and it was theirs.

This neighborhood cooperation thing that is so big these days, they had an agenda. Right now it's an unpaved parking lot that's scarcely used.

They [the college] wonder why the people are so angry. There are the little things you don't find out until later. All the owners were interested in selling to the college. They had plenty of money to buy. We all filed the papers. And what happened was that they were looking for a few specific pieces, but they had to advertise it so they wouldn't look like they were discriminating. So we went through all that for nothing. We didn't have a prayer. They only hired this company to do the advertising and take the applications.

Laura's description of this land-based conflict is one in which she perceived a power imbalance between home owners and the college. She talked about the college's access to legal support, which allowed it to buy pre-selected pieces of land without letting the home owners in on "their agenda." She believed that the college violated the neighbors' trust when they dealt unfairly with them. Laura's perception was another expression of mistrust present in Hampton's neighborhood.

Resources

You may ask why the relationship between a few of Riverton's home owners and the state college has a place in a book about a peer mediation program. The answer is this: To understand the ways in which students learn to view conflicts in school, it is essential to know something about the ways in which they learn about neighborhood conflicts. You will need to identify resources particular to your school's community and examine ways in which perceived threats to resources, such as housing, employment, or land, are communicated and handled. Consider which groups' needs are being addressed as conflicts emerge. Think about models for resolving conflicts over the community's assets and how they are understood by students, parents, neighbors, and business people.

Develop a plan to investigate conflicts over resources in your school's community by

- collecting newspaper articles;
- interviewing residents and business people in the community;
- keeping a log of local newscasts;
- gathering local and federal government demographic information;
- finding local historical books and documents.

Ask the following questions about conflict resolution patterns in your school's community:

Are community groups organized to form power bases?

Whose interests are represented when conflicts are solved?

What are your school community's chief resources?

As you gather materials about your community, such as newspaper articles, interviews, local and federal government reports, and historical documentation, ask yourself, Whose perspectives do they represent?

Are there patterns of conflict that emerge from your data?

What underlying issues seem to emerge from sources of conflict that you identify?

That's Not Nice, But People Do That

When I talked with Mandy Arles, a new fifth-grade student at Hampton, we talked about why students might not choose mediation to solve their conflict. She said, "Some people want the problem to stay and like getting into a fight. Or they don't want to take time for a mediation. Or if the other person was unpopular or rich or poor. That's not nice, but people do that."

Mandy's last statement brought up a third source of conflict: values. Gee (1990) said, "The cultural models of the student's own home culture can conflict seriously with those of mainstream culture. And some of the values of mainstream culture are complicit with the oppression of some students' home cultures" (p. 90). He theorized that "languages are *social possessions,* possessions that partly define who counts as 'real' members of the group, 'insiders'" (p. 78). If agreeing to mediation conflicted with values, then disputants might tend to discount it. It should be noted that Mandy was herself an "outsider" because she had just moved into Hampton's district from Lindenville, an affluent town that bordered Riverton. She seemed to be offering an objective view of what she was seeing in her new school.

I recalled Ricky's comment about Allison and her family's status as "renters." It could be interpreted as an example of a child's valuing home owners above renters. There were other isolating maxims I learned from Hampton students that would, if obeyed, conflict with participation in the mediation process. They were: Don't tell anyone your business, and stay out of other people's business. Looked at from a home/neighborhood perspective, disputants were being asked to tell their "business" to two peer mediators, whose school-sanctioned role was to be in their business. Mandy's statement seemed to indicate that she thought class issues might exclude some students from the process. What she seemed to be implying was that if a student had a dispute with a friend, then he or she might consider mediation. But having to sit down next to someone who was "unpopular" or not in the same economic or social class might make mediation an uncomfortable or threatening situation to be avoided.

Children learn values from family, as well as secondary social groups. Joan Carpinella talked about how much she appreciated Hampton's diverse student population:

> Last year, a Vietnamese boy in Charles' class wore a little jade Buddha. They had a discussion about what it was and why he wore it. The boy told him what it was and why he wore it. The boy told me that they did not have a temple in Riverton, but that his family had a shrine at home. I didn't have the vaguest idea of Buddhism until I was in college, and here's a kid in fourth grade who is learning about it. To me, that enriches Charles, and he is better for it.
>
> When I worked with the [new high school] debt exclusion group, I

became aware of the racism in this city, and that was something I wasn't really aware of before because it didn't touch me. My kids don't see color. That's one of the reasons why I sent them to public school. When I grew up, there were two Black families in Riverton. They were professional people, more or less. They weren't low income—there weren't as many low income people then.

In contrast to Joan's expression of liberal racial views are Laura's, whose perspective grew from having lived on Cobbler Street and then on North Star Road. She described seeing Section 8 (welfare) parenting practices:

Some conflict came from mothers fighting over their children. Screaming. They would drag their children and make them stand right there and face up to it. Or they would walk into each other's homes. Just walk right in. It got really bad, just like on TV.

There was a family who lived next door who was White. They had eight kids. The father was over seventy years old, and the mother was about thirty-five. There would be fighting and the police would come. Their kids would shoplift at the mall, get caught, and the police would bring them home. It was always something. Or they would stand on their porch and throw all their trash into the street. These were things that the parents could have stopped if they were at all concerned with what their children were doing.

Now [in her new home], we have cooperative neighbors who respect each other's property. Most of these people are from the same age group and are all white-collar. They haven't been exposed to what my family has experienced. They have no patience with it. I'm prejudiced. I can say that because I have dealt with it. When I lived in my home town, I would have been the first one to say I wasn't prejudiced. But now I've lived with these problems. My new neighbors never have.

While Laura and Joan both voiced their appreciation of Hampton Campus School's multicultural population, they recognized that many students come from families living below the poverty line. Ana, who is Hispanic, said, "I have heard people say that there are a lot of minority kids there, kids with parents on welfare. Some parents want to better themselves, so they don't want their kids there." In what could be seen as a reflection of the larger society, it appeared that the negative perceptions of some Hampton parents were more strongly linked to the values inherent in class than in race. During the 1980s, the growing number of poor people nationwide—people like those living on and around Cobbler Street—threatened the country's equilibrium and continues today to be a major irritant to the shrinking middle class. Poor residents, then, become sources of conflict not only in the areas of needs (public and personal safety), and resources (higher tax appropriations to pay for social services), but also in the area of values (religious, moral, and ethical).

Values

Consider how values are expressed in your school's community and how differences among people's values are received. Identify community-based groups and see if all groups are represented. If there are conflicts that arise from perceived threats to one group's values, how do they attempt to resolve those issues?

Ask these questions:

Are there "us-versus-them" issues over values that have polarized members of the community?

How are school districts delineated?

How might people perceive your school's neighborhoods?

A Step Back to Reflect

For over two decades, I drove in and out of Riverton and did not "know" it well enough to take on the task of implementing a peer mediation program. Until I was able to look at Hampton Campus School's community through conflict's special lenses, I could not appreciate its special qualities and how they could impact the program. The process of learning about Riverton continues each day, as I listen to the local radio station and clip articles that will help me better understand the nature of people's conflicts and the methods they use to resolve them.

Time invested in reflecting on what you already know about your school's community will be time well spent. Using the concept of conflict—more specifically, its causes (perceived threats to physical and psychological needs, resources, and values)—you can think about how to better understand students' home and neighborhood environments. Knowing about conflicts in your school's community will help you understand the ways in which the peer mediation program is being perceived and received there.

Theorist and researcher Morton Deutsch believes that conflict should be viewed positively as a natural, everyday part of our lives and as an opportunity for creative problem solving. You might find that attitude to be lacking in your school's community. As you research your school's community, you are asking two crucial questions: What kinds of conflicts do people in this community have? and How do they attempt to resolve them? Your answers will teach you about the models of conflict resolution presented to students who live there.

C H A P T E R   F O U R

≈ ≈

Understand Mediation
from the Inside

What Does a Mediator Do?

Students frequently ask, "What gave you the idea to start a peer mediation program?" The answer to that question builds a bridge to Section Two and addresses a major concern: the level of preparation I believe is necessary to take on the role of coordinator/coach.

John came home one day in the fall of 1991 with a haircut and some news: "Lillian's become a mediator." John and Lillian Comeau, a friend I hadn't seen much in two years, shared the same hairdresser, who doubled as a reliable source of information.

"What does a mediator do?"

It was a fortuitous question that would change my life.

"She mediates disputes for a local community mediation program that's affiliated with Riverton's district court. She's about to take over as director."

At the time, I was enrolled in a graduate course at the University of New Hampshire entitled "Issues and Methods in Ethnographic Research in Education." The required project involved locating a setting that was "strange" to me and making it "familiar" through observations and interviews, analysis and interpretation. I needed to study social relations by first focusing on a group or an individual in a specific setting and then analyzing the meanings that seemed to grow from people's behaviors. I would be recording their perceptions about behavior and exploring social structures or models that people kept in mind as they went about their daily activities (Spindler 1988; Wolcott 1990; Van Maanen 1988; Fetterman 1989). Wolcott (1988) explained:

> A basic tenet of descriptive research is that people in a setting do *not* necessarily "know how it is": seemingly everyday or routine behavior is worthy of scrutiny. The obvious is not so obvious after all. We want people to look more carefully, to analyze more critically, and to recognize that things are probably more rather than less complex than they seem, even as we search for ways to reduce that complexity enough to render understandable accounts. (p. 28)

This assignment was designed to provide the experiences in cultural theory building necessary for the research strand of my doctoral program. Observing a mediation program in progress seemed like a good choice for a "strange setting" because the people there were involved in a process about which I knew virtually nothing. I did not realize at the time that Wolcott's quotation was as much about understanding the role of mediator as it was about what qualitative researchers do.

A particular quotation from Jerome Bruner's (1990) *Acts of Meaning* resonated for me when I asked Lillian's permission to observe and interview her and also to approach others in the group:

> It is probably the case that human beings forever suffer conflicts of interest, with attendant grudges, factions, coalitions, and shifting alliances. But what is interesting about these fractious phenomena is not how much they separate us but how much more often they are neutralized or forgiven or excused. The primotologist Frans de Waal warns that ethnologists have tended to exaggerate the aggressiveness of primates (including . . . [human beings]) while undervaluing (and underobserving) the myriad means by which these higher species keep peace. (p. 95)

I thought, "What better group to observe than one devoted to resolving conflicts without violence or litigation?" And so, Lillian agreed to become my "intermediary . . . [and] facilitator" (Fetterman 1989, p. 43), allowing me access to people and program documents that would teach me about mediation process and show me how this group of volunteer peacemakers understood their roles inside the program. A brochure that Lillian gave me on the first day described mediation in this way:

> Mediation is a process which allows two parties to come before a neutral third party, the mediator, in hopes of finding a mutually satisfactory agreement. A mediator helps people involved in a dispute explore ways of resolving a problem by listening, guiding discussion, clarifying legal and emotional issues, setting the agenda, and writing agreements. (see Appendix A.3)

For a period spanning eight weeks, I listened to mediators "talk the talk" and began to learn how they perceived their role and how others perceived them when they participated in a ritual known as mediation. It was an experience that ushered me into a new world of language, behaviors, values, and norms. While its members wished to be perceived as being "from the community" (as they explicitly stated to disputants in their verbal introduction), mediator Discourse required "certain ways of using language, certain ways of acting and interacting, and the display of certain values and attitudes" (Gee 1990, p. xvii). What mediators seemed to know about doing their job was recognized as part of an "identity kit which comes complete with the appropriate costume and instructions on how to act, talk, and often write, so as to take on a particular social role that others will recognize" (Gee 1990, p. 142).

By the time I finished the research methods course, I knew I wanted to become a mediator.

I was drawn to mediation because it gave people guidance in solving their own conflicts. I believed that people *could and should* solve their own problems. This corresponded to mediation's principle of self-determination, "which recognizes that parties to a dispute have the ability and right to define their issues, needs and solutions and to determine the outcome of the process without advice or suggestions from staff or mediators. The parties have the final say as to the terms of any agreement reached in mediation" (Franklin Mediation Service 1991, p. 4). I wanted to learn about the process created to help others use talk, rather than an extreme response of fight or flight, to resolve conflicts.

Becoming a mediator would also satisfy a lifelong passion for learning something new; mediation process used strategies in identifying and clarifying underlying issues, actively listening, understanding multiple realities, maintaining neutrality, building trust, asking open-ended questions, gathering information, and understanding the importance of confidentiality. Learning mediation skills and strategies could make me a better, more responsive person, thinker, and teacher.

I would be investing in a belief system and process that I could teach to elementary school students. Conflict resolution and mediation offers thinkers a revised attitude toward having problems: since problems are an integral part of our lives, let's learn to manage them, not just suppress them, fight our way through them, or let someone else solve them for us. Students would receive a powerful message from the presence of a peer mediation program: adults care about us and our interpersonal problems and believe that we are capable of creating solutions ourselves.

When I began the preliminary project, I could not have predicted that the experience would become the basis for my dissertation research project and would develop into two meaningful and sustained sets of relationships—between the community mediation program, the campus school, and myself. If I was going to implement a peer mediation program and study it, I was not going to be "content to allow [myself] to be cast in the role of traditional educational researcher—the intruder who will be around for awhile and then forever disappear" (Hymes, quoted in Gilmore and Glatthorn 1982, p. 14). I would work to have the elementary peer mediation program become part of my permanent college teaching load.

My next step involved finding a basic mediation training. It was a challenge because Riverton's community program was not planning one in the near future. A call to the National Association for Mediation in Education led me to Franklin Mediation Service in Greenfield, Massachusetts. I found myself writing a check for $500 (an average fee for that time) and driving seventy miles to a private boarding school in Massachusetts' Berkshire Mountains, the site chosen for the five-day, thirty-hour basic training.

While March winds snapped the trees awake, sixteen women and eight men grouped and regrouped inside buildings that had been temporarily abandoned by students and staff on spring break. We immersed ourselves in activities that our quartet of trainers had carefully constructed to introduce us to mediation's belief system and help us learn the process from the inside.

In some ways our group of volunteer trainees was as diverse as the people from the surrounding communities we hoped to serve. We came in many shapes and various shades of Brown, Black, and White; we were of European and African descent. We were Jewish, Catholic, Protestant, Muslim, agnostic, and atheist. We were straight and gay. We were young, middle-aged, and beyond. We were funny and serious.

With respect to gender, there was a two-to-one, female-to-male ratio. I had noticed the same phenomenon when I observed Riverton's community program. It became a habit to count women and men whenever mediators gathered at conferences or regional meetings. It was usually the same or even more lopsided in favor of women. This quasi-finding made me wonder what it was about mediation that attracted women. Are mediators, with their nonadversarial, nonjudgmental demeanor rooted in receptivity, relatedness, and responsiveness, fundamentally tied to a "feminine approach" to conflict resolution? Nel Noddings, (1988), whose work in *Ethics and Moral Education* emphasized caring, relation, and response, helped me consider one possible interpretation:

> As an ethical orientation, caring has often been characterized as feminine because it seems to arise more naturally out of woman's experience than man's. When this ethical orientation is reflected on and technically elaborated, we find that it is a form of what may be called *relational ethics*. A relational ethic remains tightly tied to experience because all its deliberations focus on the human beings involved in the situation under consideration and their relations to each other. (p. 218)

Mediation, with its focus on conflict situations and people's "relations to each other," seemed at home with Noddings' feminine relational ethic. I wondered how gender issues would impact Hampton's peer mediation program. If a program were dominated by one gender, would it limit the other gender's participation?

Another issue implicit in the mediators' group makeup was connected to disputants' seeing "someone like them," a peer, guiding them through the process. I noticed that we were largely a middle-class group of social workers, lawyers, college administrators, teachers, recently graduated college students, and retired professionals looking for new territory to explore. But where were the merchants, factory workers, bus drivers, physicians, and data processors? Where were the underemployed and unemployed? My perceptions about a group's diversity (or lack of it) would affect the student mediator selection process I describe in Chapter 6. I would have to consider Hampton Campus School's population and know that peer mediators should reflect, as closely as possible, the composition of the student body with respect to ethnicity, gender, and class.

The basic training was intense, exhausting, and exhilarating. We absorbed language and processed the process by stepping in and out of mediator and disputant roles during role-play observations, role-play participation, self-esteem and bias awareness activities, discussion groups and lectures. Our coaches used methods that were designed to "teach$_a$" us mediation Discourse:

> "Teach$_a$" (with a little subscripted 'a') means to apprentice someone in a master-apprentice relationship in a social practice (Discourse) wherein you scaffold their growing ability to say, do, value, believe, within that Discourse, through demonstrating your mastery and supporting theirs even when it barely exists (i.e., you make it like they can do what they really cannot do). (Gee 1990, p. 154)

All through training, my wish to "apprentice" students in this Discourse grew stronger. Experiencing methods firsthand helped me begin to acquire a mediator Discourse and gave me insight into how I might teach students in the upcoming months. Gee (1990) gave meaning to my beginning mastery of mediation as a secondary Discourse when he stated that it "is a product of acquisition, not learning; that is, it requires exposure to models in natural, meaningful and functional settings . . ." (p. 154). It was experiential learning and reflective thinking at its best.

We watched our coaches mediate disputes in role plays based on real cases. Coaches observed us fumbling our way through first attempts to mediate simulated disputes and gave us feedback: "What information were you after when you asked that question?" "What did you notice about the first disputant's body language?" "How did you feel when you were asked that question?" We were integrating ways of using language that Gee described as the "being-doing-thinking-valuing-speaking-listening (-writing-reading)" (p. 174) combination necessary to acquiring the Discourse. In the context of mediation, "what *you are* and *do* when you say it" (p. 140) is as important as knowing how to manage the grammar of mediation. We were participating in the process, then taking time to process our participation. Our coaches were using practices that established an interactive, reflective learning environment found in some of today's classrooms (Zemelman, Daniels, and Hyde 1993).

We also became aware of the "god terms" of mediation, those "terms to which the very highest respect is paid" (Weaver, quoted in Newkirk 1989, p. 179); the following linguistic quintet became the hub of our understanding all that we represented:

1. self-determination
2. informed consent
3. confidentiality
4. voluntariness
5. impartiality/neutrality

Each mediation is a separate, complex, and powerful event that finds its life within these five principles. When I considered the ways in which each principle would be applied in a school's peer mediation program, questions collected around them, like metal shavings attracted to the ends of magnets.

While I believed in students' rights and abilities to solve their own problems, I wondered in what ways the system of discipline at Hampton Campus School would support or conflict with a belief in "self-determination." Would staff, parents, and students view mediation as "a way out of going to the office" for "justice"? Would students who had used violence in a dispute be permitted to choose mediation *instead of* seeing the assistant principal, Mr. Reynolds? Would students see themselves as capable of settling their own in-school disputes if they were encultured to automatically turn to adults for help?

Informed consent "is the principle which affirms the parties' right to information about the mediation process, their legal rights and legal and social service options before consenting to participate in mediation or to the terms of any agreement reached in mediation" (Franklin Mediation Service 1991, p. 4). In a school's peer mediation program, it meant—in order to guarantee that students would know enough about mediation to accept or reject it on the first day peer mediators went on duty—I would need to plan several meetings and share information about mediation months in advance with the following people:

- superintendent of schools
- president of the college
- principal
- assistant principal
- teachers
- staff
- parent-teacher organization

Cohen (1987a) pointed out that "Change within organizations does not come easily and schools are no exception . . . Experts agree that the most essential requirement for organizational change to be successful is the support of the people who control the organization" (p. 1). On March 13, I met for the first time with Hampton's principal, Dr. Richard Camden, and explained how a peer mediation program might look in Hampton, as well as what my role as coordinator/trainer/researcher would be. On April 9, Dr. Camden accompanied me to a meeting with Dr. James Malone, Riverton State College's president. On June 9, I found myself assuring Riverton's superintendent that "No, the peer mediation program will not replace the discipline system or undermine Jim Reynolds' authority." I promised administrators, teachers, and parents that students involved in mediations, either as disputants or mediators, would be doing so at lunch and recess and therefore, not be losing "instructional time." The principle of informed consent became one that required sharing information about the intended program's design, as well as teaching about the philosophy behind mediation process.

Confidentiality "is the principle which guarantees that all information received from the parties will be kept within the Program, in order that parties will feel free to explore the issues and potential solutions. Any exceptions to this guarantee shall be made clear to the parties prior to their consent to participate in mediation" (Franklin Mediation Service 1991, p. 4). Adult mediators cannot be subpoenaed in court and are required to destroy any notes taken during the mediation. Mediators also state during the introduction that "everything we say here is confidential." Would students be able to trust each other enough to enter into a mediation? I would need to think about how peer mediators would build that trust and communicate their ability to keep information confidential. Who would have copies of each agreement? Disputants? Parents? The assistant principal?

Voluntariness "is the principle which acknowledges the parties' right to freely enter into both the mediation process and any agreement reached in that process. The parties have a right to withdraw from mediation at any time" (p. 4). This meant that if any coercion were suspected through reading body language or hearing explicit or implicit statements, the mediation would have to be stopped. Implications for a school program were that adult volunteers screening disputes and peer mediators would need to assess disputants' voluntary participation.

Neutrality "is the principle which affirms the parties' right to a process that serves all parties fairly and equally and to mediators who refrain from perceived or actual bias or favoritism, either by word or deed" (p. 4). How would I be able to teach fourth- and fifth-grade students this concept? How would they understand the part it played in the mediation process?

My training continued with its text and subtext. Lectures and activities helped us identify conflict styles, heighten our awareness of cultural differences and personal biases, and increase our understanding of empathy. We practiced mediator skills—reframing conflict narratives, restating emotions, identifying underlying issues and positives, recognizing power imbalances, asking open-ended and clarifying questions, separating wants from needs, helping disputants generate options, acting as an agent of reality, and writing balanced agreements (Fisher, Ury, and Patten 1991; Franklin Mediation Service 1991).

Throughout our training, we exchanged questions with our coaches and each other. We considered answers. We asked more questions. We coalesced into a team, albeit a temporary one.

I filled a large notebook during those hours and days of training as I tried to capture ideas. Joe Lieberman, a community college dean, leaned over at one point and said to me: "I never saw anyone write as fast or as much as you do." What he did not know was that I was acquiring this new Discourse with the specific purpose of adding it to another group's repertoire: fourth- and fifth-grade students.

After my basic training, I asked Lillian to take me into Riverton's community court mediation program as an intern. It meant that I would volunteer to co-mediate at least three cases. Between June and August, I co-mediated four disputes either in the lawyers' conference room in Riverton's district court house or in an unoccupied school across the street from a police station/court house in Lincoln.

I found myself gripping the steering wheel tightly on the twenty-five mile drive home from mediations, barely hearing music that was usually as important to me as gasoline was to the car. I was reminded of I. A. Richards' metaphor of ambiguities as "the hinges of thought" (Berthoff 1981, p. 75) when I found my mind weighing each set of meanings from several points of view.

How could I feel empathy toward a plaintiff in a property damage dispute whose list of grievances during a private session included a snide, "You know, he *loved* his [male] roommate"? How could I step into the shoes of a fifteen-year-old defendant who rolled her eyes at me in an Archie Bunker-like expression when the plaintiff she had assaulted translated everything into Spanish for her mother? A mediator suspends judgment and steps into each disputant's reality, even when it is homophobic or racist.

I recalled reading David Fetterman's (1989) response to the "demands of personal tolerance and trust" when he realized while interviewing a sweet, friendly German immigrant in a senior citizen day-care center that she was "not a victim but a supporter of the Nazi movement." Fetterman wrote: "This ethical balancing act was one of the most difficult I have had to maintain as an ethnographer" (p. 133). When I read Fetterman's description, I empathized as a mediator. I realized then that trust building, neutrality, and empathy were going to be more complex and challenging than I had expected.

Another of mediation's "god terms" came into question that summer as my partners and I co-mediated disputes. How could I not be suspicious when the defendant in a minor criminal case let it slip that she had "done this before"? By *voluntarily* choosing mediation and fulfilling her side of the agreement, this case would not come before a judge. How many times had she used mediation to avoid a conviction?

Other issues emerged during mediations. How could I deal with feeling that my co-mediator was dominating me? We were supposed to be modeling cooperation for disputants. Did his treatment of me have to do with my relative lack of experience? Or was it gender-related? Hanisch and Carnevale (1987) found that male college students projecting themselves into the role of "mediator were more forceful, more confident, and believed that their efforts were more influential than females" (p. 7), who were more inactive "which involves letting the disputants handle the controversy on their own" (p. 4). Suppose that my perception of his dominance was linked to gender differences. Didn't a belief in self-determination support the feminine response to a mediator's placement in the mediation process?

I raise these questions now because they surfaced during my own initiation and immersion in the mediation process. I believe that *without actually facing these problems and dilemmas myself, I would have had a limited understanding of and little appreciation for what students would be dealing with in the months ahead.* I could practice conflict resolution skills and strategies in my personal life and teach my college Language Arts students about mediation's benefits (Finn 1993, Chapter 4). I could recognize and analyze sources of conflict as I worked in the campus school and investigated its neighborhoods. But, until I actually mediated disputes and tried to tease out underlying issues or until I struggled to see a problem from each point of view, until I felt the challenges to my neutral stance as I listened to disputants in private or joint sessions, I could not ask students to do the same.

Preparation

It may be surprising to learn that the purpose of this chapter is not to convince you to become trained as a mediator and volunteer in your local community program. A commitment to study and uphold the five principles of mediation must come from a set of highly personal decisions. My purpose is something more crucial: to help you understand *the ethical need* for adults to be sufficiently prepared before involving students as mediators and disputants.

There can be varying levels of preparation necessary to take on a new role. If we adults believe in the promise of mediation enough to bring the experience to students, then we also have a moral obligation to be well prepared in what we are doing. Basic training, including an internship, can be the foundation of that commitment. To take this issue one step further would mean volunteering in a community mediation program or working in a collaborative relationship between school and community programs.

My concern over basic levels of preparation stems from current pressure on school administrators to quell violence in schools. In "The Fourth R," The National Association for Mediation in Education newsletter, editors speculated that the 40 percent increase in membership in 1992—from 685 to 968—was "due to exploding national interest in the field of peer mediation and conflict resolution" (Townley 1993, p. 6). However, this widespread sense of urgency may result in an underprepared or uncommitted staff responding to one more top-down decision. It is similar to the situation discussed in Chapter 2 with respect to conflict resolution curriculum being handed from administrators to staff.

As mediation takes hold in the wider culture, resources grow to meet the demand for information. Your quest for high-quality preparation that meets recommended standards (see Appendixes A.4, A.5) will likely be several phone calls or letters away. National and regional organizations that will help to locate trainings, publications, conferences, and access to other resources are listed in Appendix A.6.

It seems that there is a fundamental need to explore issues situated at a personal level, at the heart of one's motivation, to learn what it means to become a mediator. The following questions helped me to examine the issue of personal commitment:

> What do I know and believe about mediation that makes it seem like a viable alternative to current methods of conflict resolution used in the school?
>
> What will I achieve by becoming a mediator?
>
> What will motivate me to learn more about mediation?
>
> How do the principles of mediation fit my worldview?
>
> How will I learn about the role of mediator?

A Step Back to Reflect

Every summer, my husband, John, and I take a week's vacation in Wellfleet on Cape Cod, Massachusetts. Our regular rounds include Herridge's, a used bookstore dappled in shade and drenched in quaintness. Its books rest on shelves labeled with delicate, hand-lettered signs, such as "Literature," "Philosophy/Religion," and "Eastern Thought." We spend hours stooping or reaching for books, then fitting ourselves in any of several worn wooden chairs placed among the plants and tables.

During our August 1992 visit, I was thumbing through *Mirror of the Heart: Poems of Sara Teasdale* (Teasdale 1984) when I came across "Duty." I found myself rereading it because it seemed to speak to me about my choice to step into other people's problems through mediation. Teasdale's poem became a source of inspiration for this book, and I use it now to help me end this first section. It may clarify why it took four chapters to explore ethical and educational issues that I believe are necessary to consider *before* starting up a peer mediation program.

> DUTY
>
> Fool, do not beat the air
>   With miserable hands—
> The wrong is done, the seed is sown,
>   The evil stands.
>
> Your duty is to draw
>   Out of the web of wrong,
> Out of ill-woven deeds,
>   A thread of song.

The poem brought to mind the work of Nel Noddings, and I thought, if she had written this poem, she might have named it "Caring." Teasdale's choice of "duty" would resonate with tones of traditional Kantian ethics which "insisted that only those acts performed out of duty (in conformity to principle) should be labeled moral, [whereas] an ethic of caring prefers acts done out of love and natural inclination. Acting out of caring, one calls on a sense of duty or special obligation only when love or inclination fails" (Noddings 1988, p. 219).

Teasdale's poem spoke to me the same way that Nel Noddings' relational ethics did as I learned about the mediation process. Both made me realize that starting a peer mediation program in an elementary school had much to do with how I felt about students after thirty years of teaching. In a section headed, "Caring as a Moral Orientation in Teaching," Noddings wrote,

> A relation . . . is construed as any pairing or connection of individuals characterized by some affective awareness in each. It is an encounter or series of encounters in which the involved parties feel something toward each other. Relations may be characterized by love or hate, anger or sorrow, admiration or envy; or, of course, they may reveal mixed affects— one party feeling, say, love and the other revulsion. One who is concerned with behaving ethically strives always to preserve or convert a given relation into a caring relation. (pp. 218–19)

I saw in Noddings and Teasdale the same emphasis on caring and laying open the roots of past feelings and events that hampered the development of relationships. Noddings and Teasdale not only described a context and motivation for an ethic of teaching, but accounted for an ethic of caring that emerged from students when a peer mediation program began at Hampton Campus School.

SECTION TWO

≈≈≈≈≈≈≈≈≈≈≈≈≈≈≈≈≈≈≈≈≈≈≈

Starting Up a Peer Mediation Program

CHAPTER FIVE

≈ ≈

Seeking Volunteers

It's Kind of Like Being a Researcher

During the first week of January 1993, I began a week-long schedule of forty-five minute presentations by pushing a cart into eight fourth- and fifth-grade classrooms. I opted for a series of individual classroom presentations to seek volunteers instead of grade-level or school assemblies because I felt that large group assemblies could be impersonal. Classrooms might provide a more relaxed, interactive setting for students, and so I made arrangements with teachers during their December team meetings.

I knocked at each door prepared with a video, a VCR, three pieces of chart paper, and high hopes, but no assurances that students would subscribe to "the promise of mediation" in their school. My assumption was that there would be at least some who would want to step into this new Discourse with me because they understood the need for it, saw mediation as a possible alternative to Hampton's established patterns of conflict resolution, and wanted to voluntarily step into the role.

After each teacher introduced me, I wrote my name and these words on the chalkboard: teacher, mediator, coordinator/trainer, researcher. Students watched quietly from their seats, while their teacher settled into a chair or behind a large, green desk.

"I'm here today to tell you about a new program that I'll be starting up at Hampton. I hope that some of you might be interested in it, too." I pointed to the chalkboard. "It involves these jobs I've chosen to do." A boy raised his hand, and I nodded, "Yes, Eric."

"We going to see a movie?"

"No. Well, actually, about four minutes from one video." I asked students to predict what it might be about. Hands went up.

"Conflict?"

The response made me think about how working with Clare Riley during their guidance activity period for the past three months had established a specific identity for me. "Any other predictions?"

"Problem solving?"

"Where's Miss Riley? Is she going to do this, too?"

I told students that the new program did involve conflict, but I would be the only coordinator/trainer. "I am an adult mediator who wants to see if some students might be interested in volunteering for a new program. If you are, then

I will be training you. We'll work together to build a peer mediation program at Hampton. Miss Riley will still be doing conflict resolution lessons during your regular guidance period, and what you learn then will really help you if you choose to get involved in a mediation."

I cued the VCR to a four-minute peer mediation role play from the twenty-three minute video, "Peacemakers of the Future" (Bankier and Dondlinger 1991). Because I had forty-five minutes for each presentation, I made the decision to bypass a series of adult experts talking about the value of having an in-school program. This segment featured elementary students in the roles of peer mediators and disputants. It might be the first time they would see or hear terms such as mediation, mediator, dispute, and disputant. If this video was the students' first look at the process, they would be seeing a model of a "prototypical (what we take to be 'normal') event" (Gee 1990, p. 87) known as mediation.

While the elementary mediation role-play segment *did show* the steps of the process, its four-minute length *did not allow* students to see peer mediators guide disputants through time-consuming clarifying questions or brainstorming and negotiating their way to a final agreement. Imperfect as it seemed from a mediator's point of view, I considered students' perspectives and asked myself, "Does this segment demonstrate the basic steps of the mediation process to students who may not have a broad knowledge base?" I felt that it did.

"I'd like you to pay special attention to what the two boys in the video are doing." I observed students as their faces switched to a trancelike television-watching mode; they watched two boys and two girls who sat grouped around a table in an unoccupied classroom. Each pair had one African American and one Anglo-American. The words "Elementary School Mock Mediation" appeared for a few seconds at the bottom of the screen. A fair-skinned boy wearing glasses began:

> *Patrick:* Hello, my name is Patrick. This is Rashad. And you are? [He gestures toward the girls.]
>
> *Sarah* [a light brown-haired girl with luminous blue eyes]: Sarah.
>
> *Nubian* [a brown-skinned girl whose face is framed by a halo of black hair. She manages to sustain the offended air of a plaintiff from the start]: Nubian.
>
> *Patrick:* We are trained to help you solve your problem. Nubian, do you *want* to solve your problem?
>
> *Nubian:* Yes.
>
> *Patrick* [elicits the same response from Sarah when he asks her the same question and then proceeds]: Before we begin, we need to get an agreement from each person for these five ground rules. [He asks each girl] Do you agree to solve the problem? [After they agree, he continues.] Do you agree to no name-calling, put-downs, or physical fighting?
>
> *Rashad* [takes over at this point and asks each girl]: Do you agree to be as honest as you can? [When they both agree, he finishes the introduction.] We, as mediators, agree not to talk to others about this mediation. Everything said here is confidential, except for things about drugs, weapons, alcohol, or touching on private parts.

Patrick [takes over again]: Nubian, you brought up the problem, so you speak first.

Nubian: This new girl, Ariel, came to school, okay, and me and Sarah were supposed to be best friends, but all of a sudden, she started playing with *her* and, like, she left me out.

Sarah [interrupts]: No, I didn't!

Nubian [snaps back]: Yes, you did!

Patrick [off camera]: SShhhh! Nubian, anything else?

Nubian: No, that's it.

Patrick [restates]: So, what you're saying is that when this new girl, Ariel, came to school, Sarah was playing with her and wasn't playing with you anymore? [He waits for Nubian's "Yes."] And you felt left out? [She nods.] And how does that make you feel?

Nubian: Real mad!

Patrick: Why does it make you feel that way?

Nubian: She's supposed to be my best friend. She's supposed to play with me!

Rashad [takes over]: Sarah, from your point of view, what happened?

Sarah: Well, when Ariel came to school, she was being left out of everything, so I started being her friend. And I didn't mean to leave Nubian out of anything.

Nubian [interjects]: Yeah, right.

Patrick [firmly]: Nubian, you agreed not to interrupt. (Bankier and Dondlinger 1991)

When Patrick and Rashad restated the conflict, I heard Lashawna Winslow, an outspoken African-American girl, snort, "What's he saying it *again* for? Didn't he *just hear her say that?*" She could have been noticing the same mismatch that Terry Cortez had (see Chapter 2). I observed girls making eye contact with other girls in the room; they could have been connecting Sarah and Nubian's problem to one that they may have had.

Rashad and Patrick asked both girls to restate the problem from the opposite point of view, and then asked for a public position from each one: "What do you want from this problem?" Sarah and Nubian each responded to "What can *you* do now to solve the problem?" and heard Patrick restate their solutions, while Rashad wrote the agreement. Patrick asked both girls, "What can you do differently in the future?" Nubian said that she would "talk to Sarah" and Sarah said that she would ask her why she wasn't playing with her anymore. The mediation ended. "Tell your friends the problem has been solved so that they won't spread rumors. You did a good job!" All four shook hands vigorously.

"What did Patrick and Rashad do in this scene?" I asked.

Hands shot up. "Rodney?"

"Helped the girls solve their problem."

"Who came up with the solutions?" Fewer hands went up as they turned the scene over in their minds. "Cathy?"

"Nubian and Sarah did."

"Why not Patrick or Rashad?"

A long wait . . . then I prompted, "Whose problem is it? Tony."

"The girls'! It's not the boys' problem."

"How did the peer mediators help, then?" More hands. That seemed easier. "Paul."

"They asked Sarah and Nubian questions about the problem."

"Why do you suppose they did that?" Kristi Tesadore tipped back in her chair with an "I just figured out a good way to think about this" expression lighting up her brown eyes. It was a look that I would come to appreciate. "Kristi?"

"It's kind of like being a researcher."

I admired Kristi's ability to see a relationship between the thinking skills that drive both processes. "What do you mean, Kristi?"

"Well, first of all, you look at the problem. You find out as much as you can by asking questions. And then they think up some things to try out that will solve the problem."

"It makes sense to think about it that way, Kristi. It sounds to me as if you are describing a team of researchers. You saw the peer mediators go through a series of steps with the disputants to help solve the problem."

I attached a chart to the chalkboard with magnets (Figure 5.1). Students reconstructed the mediation by recalling what Patrick, Rashad, Nubian, and Sarah said during each of the five steps: introduction, description of the conflict, brainstorming solutions, making resolutions, and wrap-up.

"Can we think about some conflicts students have experienced in school that could have been talked out in mediation?" They brainstormed a list of problems, while I wrote them on the chalkboard: broken friendships, unkept promises, rumor spreading, property disputes, name-calling, teasing, and threats.

"It's important for you to know that Mr. Reynolds and I have agreed that conflicts involving physical violence are not mediatable and will still go to him."

"What do you think the word 'peer' has to do with mediation?" In many classes, students had to work through a definition of this unfamiliar term. I prompted, "I'm a peer mediator whenever I mediate disputes with other adults." Some fourth- and fifth-grade students connected to a concept they knew. Elaine Lindquist reasoned, "When I first heard it, I thought it was like peer pressure, that it was going to be people under pressure."

"'Peer' means that mediations will involve only Hampton students who will be mediators and disputants like Nubian, Sarah, Patrick, and Rashad. Peer mediation will not involve grown-ups. So, if there is a conflict between you and a teacher or another adult, you won't be able to come to mediation." Some students looked at me, others at their teacher.

"Let's talk for a few minutes about students who volunteer to become peer mediators." At that point, I clipped a second piece of chart paper to the chalkboard. For the next ten minutes, students talked their way to understanding the list of qualities that mediators needed to possess:

- They were believed to be *neutral* and able to separate the problem from a disputant who might be their "best friend or worst enemy."
- They were thought of as *fair,* and therefore able to determine whether an agreement was balanced and if both sides were doing something to solve the problem.
- They could be trusted to keep what was said in mediations *confidential.*

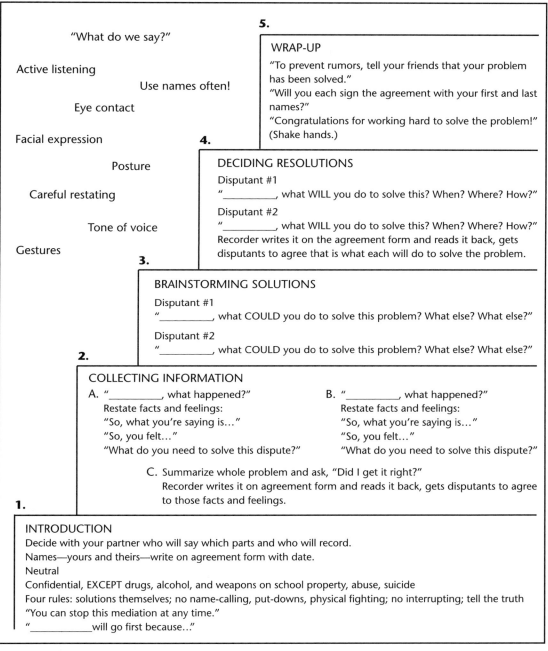

"What do we say?"

Active listening

Use names often!

Eye contact

Facial expression

Posture

Careful restating

Tone of voice

Gestures

5.

WRAP-UP
"To prevent rumors, tell your friends that your problem has been solved."
"Will you each sign the agreement with your first and last names?"
"Congratulations for working hard to solve the problem!" (Shake hands.)

4.

DECIDING RESOLUTIONS
Disputant #1
"_____, what WILL you do to solve this? When? Where? How?"
Disputant #2
"_____, what WILL you do to solve this? When? Where? How?"
Recorder writes it on the agreement form and reads it back, gets disputants to agree that is what each will do to solve the problem.

3.

BRAINSTORMING SOLUTIONS
Disputant #1
"_____, what COULD you do to solve this problem? What else? What else?"
Disputant #2
"_____, what COULD you do to solve this problem? What else? What else?"

2.

COLLECTING INFORMATION
A. "_____, what happened?"
Restate facts and feelings:
"So, what you're saying is…"
"So, you felt…"
"What do you need to solve this dispute?"

B. "_____, what happened?"
Restate facts and feelings:
"So, what you're saying is…"
"So, you felt…"
"What do you need to solve this dispute?"

C. Summarize whole problem and ask, "Did I get it right?"
Recorder writes it on agreement form and reads it back, gets disputants to agree to those facts and feelings.

1.

INTRODUCTION
Decide with your partner who will say which parts and who will record.
Names—yours and theirs—write on agreement form with date.
Neutral
Confidential, EXCEPT drugs, alcohol, and weapons on school property, abuse, suicide
Four rules: solutions themselves; no name-calling, put-downs, physical fighting; no interrupting; tell the truth
"You can stop this mediation at any time."
"_____will go first because…"

Figure 5.1 Steps in a Mediation

Peer Mediation Program Nomination

- Think about the characteristics a peer mediator needs to have:

____fair ____neutral ____dependable ____able to keep a secret

____a good listener ____ honest ____ willing to help others solve problems

- Consider whether or not you would be interested in volunteering to become a peer mediator.

_____ Yes, I am interested in becoming a peer mediator and would like to be interviewed.

_____ No, I would not be interested in becoming a peer mediator.

Your name _____ Date _____

- These are the names of other students who I think would make effective peer mediators:

_____

_____

_____

_____

Figure 5.2   Peer Mediation Program Nomination

- They were thought of as *honest.*
- They could learn to be *good listeners.*
- They were thought of as *dependable* and hard-working.
- They were *willing to help* people solve their problems.

Our discussion of mediator qualities used the open-ended questioning pattern: "What does it mean when a person is . . .?" "Can you think of a time when you were . . .?" "Why do you suppose it would be important for a peer mediator to be . . .?"

Next, students looked at the third chart, which presented terms of the commitment necessary for volunteering to become trained as a mediator:

- Students needed to attend a two-day basic training workshop.
- Peer mediators would be required to attend an after-school program every Thursday from 2:00 until 3:30 to continue training by participating in activities that would improve their skills as mediators.
- Two pairs of peer mediators would be scheduled for duty first and second lunch and recess periods, which meant that mediators would have to give up one or two recesses a week until the close of school in June.

- Peer mediators would become part of my research project. I explained that I would be studying how they were using talk to understand what mediation was about and that our after-school program would be videotaped so that I would have a record of our discussions.

"What two days? Will we miss school?"

"Your teachers have agreed to release peer mediators from regular class for two days of training on January 14 and 15. Your parents will need to agree to that, also. I will send a permission letter home if you volunteer and are selected (Appendix A.7)."

"Do we have to come to the after-school program?"

"Yes, that's required as part of your training. What we can do in ten hours over two days will be just a beginning. Even adult mediators need to attend advanced trainings in order to improve our skills."

Finally, students filled out a volunteer/nomination form (Figure 5.2) which allowed me to interview them at lunchtime during the next few days if they checked off "Yes" (Figure 5.3). I asked them to nominate any other fourth- or fifth-grade students whom they thought had the qualities we discussed.

"Does it have to be someone in this room?"

"No. If you think that someone in another fourth- or fifth-grade classroom here at Hampton would be someone you would trust to mediate your disputes, then write that person's name down."

"What if we write a person's name, but he or she doesn't volunteer?"

"If a person doesn't volunteer, then I won't be interviewing him or her. But if he or she does volunteer, then I'll know that you felt that person would make a good mediator. You know each other better than I do, and these students will be *your* peer mediators. Names that you write down will help me begin to select a group."

"You mean that everyone who volunteers won't get to be a mediator?"

"That's right. Since I am working alone to start the program, I'll be looking for about twenty-five fourth- and fifth-grade students to begin. Today, your nominations will be one of the most important ways I will have of knowing which students *you* want to see as Hampton's first peer mediators."

When I passed out the student nominating form, I gave each teacher a separate paper with the heading "These are fourth- and fifth-grade students who I think could become successful peer mediators" and asked them to take some time to nominate students.

After I collected them, I drew a grid on the chalkboard to show more about the selection process (Figure 5.4). "As I finish these classroom visits, I make a chart that gives me some information that I will need to select a group if I have more than twenty-five people volunteering from all fourth and fifth grades. I draw a line next to each name for every nomination. I'm interested in seeing where that nomination came from, so I draw four boy-girl columns: in-class, out-of-class fourth-grade student, out-of-class fifth-grade student, and teacher. So, looking at this chart and reading notes that I make during volunteer interviews are two of the ways that I hope to get a good picture of whom to select."

Peer Mediator Interview Form

Date _____ Volunteer's name _____ M / F

Grade _____ Interviewed by _____

1. What do you think will make you a good peer mediator?

2. Are you willing *and able* to give up your recess and eating lunch with your friends when you are scheduled for mediation duty?

3. Can you come to the after-school program *every* Thursday from 2:00–3:30 to learn more about being a mediator? Can you think of anything that might interfere with your being able to attend every session?

   How will you get home?
   _____ I will get picked up.
   _____ I will need to ride the after-school bus.

4. Are you willing to commit to volunteering for *one school year, through June?*

5. Tell about what or who made you decide that you wanted to volunteer to be a peer mediator.

Figure 5.3   Peer Mediator Interview Form

By the end of eight classroom presentations, I had sorted the self-nomination papers and counted 62 student volunteers out of a group totaling 150 students (41 percent). There were 39 girls and 23 boys (approximately a two-to-one ratio of girls to boys).

Presenting the Model

On the surface, outreach presentations are opportunities to seek volunteers and teach students, teachers, or parents what it means to bring a dispute to mediation. However, I learned that there are several underlying issues present in what seemed to be a fairly straightforward piece of the implementation process.

Mediator Nomination Grid

Suggestion: Color-code nomination markings to indicate gender of nominator.

Homeroom Teacher _____

Name	In-class Nomination	Out-of-class Nomination	Teacher Nomination

Figure 5.4   Mediator Nomination Grid

Outreach presentations for students begin with administrative and staff support. The road to students is paved with efforts to communicate with adults who are responsible for planning their schedules. I found this to be especially important during the implementation stage. That means negotiating times for assemblies or classroom presentations with *all* staff. Even if teachers and administrators initially support a peer mediation program by *saying,* "That's a good idea," what amounts to agreeing to an interruption in a pre-planned teaching day requires a high level of commitment (Cohen 1987a). What seems to be a matter of courtesy and common sense may be less a matter of practice in some schools. Even if your role in the school has been established prior to this time, the length and quality of your welcome will be at the discretion of teachers and administrators. Meeting with teachers and administrators gave me the opportunity to get input and cooperation on planned volunteering, training, and induction ceremony dates. The following questions guided me through this stage:

> Have I established ties to teachers, administrators, and parents that will enable me to reach students with information about the peer mediation program?
> How might students perceive me in the role of coordinator/trainer?
> What are the details of the model that I will present to students?
> What problems can I anticipate?

Volunteering is a social act. You ask students during outreach presentations to volunteer as peer mediators and to acquire a new Discourse, while you "teach$_a$" (Gee 1990, p. 154) them. However, volunteering is a social act within the context of a school's culture. What underlying meanings begin to form around the identities of peer mediator and disputant when establishing a new group in a school?

How will students' decision to volunteer or not be perceived by others? Most students want to be perceived as "normal." Particularly at the implementation stage, it is unknown where the roles of peer mediator and disputant will fit in—"risky," "normal," or "safe"—on the social scale present in social settings. Even though it is recommended that peer mediators be selected from students with a wide range of abilities and backgrounds, students could perceive peer mediators as an elite group, somewhat akin to being in the "top reading group," with its hierarchically inspired snobbery.

Another question emerged as I thought about students faced with this opportunity to volunteer. Would a student's decision augment a generally positive or negative image within the school (see Chapter 2 for more details on school culture)? In the days following the presentations, occasionally teachers would stop me and ask about particular students: "Did . . . volunteer?" followed by "Because this would do him (or her) a world of good." or a sardonic "No? It figures." A troubled student's act of volunteering (or not) could be interpreted by teachers and administrators as a step toward change or a validation of their continued resistance. I wondered about assumptions teachers might be making about the act of volunteering while they watched students hunched over their nominating forms.

Mediation is a social situation. Mediators depend on disputants. They take on a role that exists only because of the interdependent relationship between them and disputants; without disputants who are willing to become a member of the Discourse and "speak and act, and at least appear to think and feel, in terms of these values and viewpoints while being in the Discourse" (Gee 1990, p. 144), there will be no program. This means that participants must practice mediation by first subscribing to a philosophy that includes belief in self-determination, confidentiality, and neutrality (even if your "best friend or worst enemy is sitting across from you," as one student put it). Volunteering to take on a responsible role that shows they care about others is basic to a peer mediator's "identity kit"; trusting peer mediators and the process enough to voluntarily bring your dispute to them is no less important. As you design your outreach presentation, it is important to stress that all students are potential volunteers for the program because of their willingness to step into both mediator and disputant roles.

This idea returns us to the issue of conflict resolution curriculum forming an experiential base for all students (see Chapter 2). There is no question in my mind that teaching conflict resolution and negotiation skills and strategies to all students, with or without the presence of a peer mediation program, is a positive investment in the future of students. Experiences in both areas will empower students if they choose to step inside the mediation process. A seemingly ideal solution is posed by Johnson and Johnson (1991), who recommend that schools train all students as mediators:

> While the teacher may mediate conflicts among students, the teacher may also train all students to be mediators, each day (or week) select a pair of class mediators, and then refer to them all conflicts. It is important that

all students are given the opportunity to be a mediator as it will increase students' negotiation skill. Peer mediation gives students an opportunity to resolve their disputes themselves, in mutually satisfactory ways without having to engage the attention of a teacher. This empowers the students who sometimes feel like they are victims of the "arbitrary" whims of the teacher. It also reduces demands on the teacher, who can devote less time to arbitration and discipline in general, and more time to teaching. (pp. 1:14, 15)

There are differing perspectives on training all students. Cahill (1989) stated, "Not everyone who wants to be a peer mediator is cut out for it. Though NAME believes in tapping a wide range of students (troublemakers and gang leaders have been found to be surprisingly adept at handling conflict) some youngsters just don't have the capacity to remain nonjudgmental in a squabble." While I believe that one's "capacity" can be enlarged through educative experiences (Dewey [1938] 1963), I think that there is a need to pose another question relative to training *every student* to be a peer mediator: Will every student (or adult, for that matter) want to become a mediator? This question stems from my belief that students should *make the decision* to volunteer as peer mediators. I was reminded of a quotation from *The Call of Service: A Witness to Idealism* when Robert Coles (1993) shares a letter from his mother: "We all make [mistakes], blunder our way along. But we can step out of ourselves, now and then; we can take the hands of others and walk with them" (p. 287). In an ideal world, everyone might volunteer to take on the role of mediator. From a realistic perspective, not everyone will have the interest or desire to become a peer mediator. For some coordinators and trainers, it becomes a matter of dedication, acceptance of a belief system, and a commitment that not every student will be ready to make.

Communicating with Parents

As I moved closer to the selection and training phases of implementing the program, I was concerned because only a dozen parents had attended the special parents night presentation on January 6. The PTO voted their financial support by giving money to pay for the oversized plain blue tee shirts I planned to have peer mediators wear when they went on duty. I thought about the hundreds of parents who were not going to know about the program.

When so few parents attended the January meeting, I expressed my concern to Bonnie Pearson, president of the PTO. She reasoned that parents were just getting over the holidays and that, typically, after the initial fall meeting, PTO attendance dropped. I recalled the September meeting when I made a brief presentation: there were three times as many people crowded into the faculty room. While Bonnie and I talked, it made me remember something else I knew about Hampton's culture from my years as a third- and fourth-grade teacher there: parents, except for a small core group, did not attend the monthly meetings.

It would be important to think about other ways to publicize the new peer mediation program if parents were going to understand it. Peer mediation is not yet a widely recognized activity, such as soccer or basketball, and very likely not part of parents' school experience. I wondered how parents might react to their child saying, "I volunteered to be a peer mediator today." What would parents' response be to "I had a problem at school today and went to peer mediation"?

Another avenue of communication I attempted was writing notices and brief articles about peer mediation in Hampton's monthly newsletter. Before school one morning shortly after the January PTO meeting, I met Carol Avelon, a former junior high student of mine, rushing to work after meeting with her son's teacher. We talked for a few minutes in the corridor, and I mentioned the peer mediation program. She seemed surprised, so I told her that there had been some information about it in the newsletter. "Oh, that! I don't have time to wade through a seven- or eight-page booklet." Even though I continue to believe in communication using school newsletters, that day I was skeptical about how much parents would know, and therefore be able to accept, about the new program.

Experience has taught me the importance of parents' learning about mediation at the program implementation stage (see Chapter 9). As peer mediation programs become more widespread, it may be easier to assume that parents will understand what to expect. A fledgling program will do better if a diverse group of parents support it. I used some of the strategies listed below after the program was under way, but now see that I needed to try them sooner.

- Ask members of the school community to share avenues of communication with parents that they have found to be most effective.
- If sports events have good parental attendance in your school, arrange to set up a table and be there with handouts explaining peer mediation.
- Approach neighborhood organizations and offer to make brief presentations about the new peer mediation program.
- Contact local radio talk show hosts, newspaper editors, and cable television access channels who may support projects by featuring interviews with school and community members.

A Step Back to Reflect

A few months after the initial volunteer outreach presentations, a peer mediator asked, "When you came into our classroom that first time, did you worry no one would want to volunteer?" I readily admitted that I did, and "could only hope some students might think mediation would work to help others talk out their conflicts."

As you begin this phase of implementing a peer mediation program, you strum a chord—"a thread of song"—that is rooted in language some students hear and respond to. Even during the *first* classroom presentations, I noticed shifts in language as students' references to "the problem" became "the dispute" and "the boys" (Patrick and Rashad) became "the peer mediators" and "the girls" (Nubian and Sarah) became "the disputants."

Seeking volunteers becomes a different experience the second, third, and fourth time around. Hampton's peer mediators decided to make their own video and replace Rashad, Nubian, Sarah, and Patrick. When I make classroom presentations now, I begin by saying, "Before we look at the video, let's make a list of what a video about mediation will probably have in it." I write the words "Mediation is . . ." at the top of blank chart paper and watch it fill with students' perceptions.

Now when I ask, "Where did you learn so much about mediation?" the responses include, "My sister [or brother, cousin, friend] is [or was] a peer mediator." "I used mediation to solve a problem."

CHAPTER SIX

≈ ≈

Selecting Peer Mediators

Did I Make It Into Your Club?

When I walked through Hampton's corridors and into the cafeteria during the classroom outreach presentation days, I noticed that more students initiated eye contact with me. A fourth-grade girl, whom I recognized from the nomination papers as a volunteer, tried so hard to smile and maintain eye contact while she lined up for lunch that she collided with the student standing in front of her. Her not-so-subtle, nonverbal campaigning made me remember students from decades ago calling out, "Pick me! Let me help!" (see Chapter 2).

Several students stopped me in the hall or cafeteria to say, "I was going to volunteer, but I have karate (or gymnastics or baby-sitting) on Thursdays and can't stay for the after-school program." I thought that might be another way of saying, "A peer mediation program at Hampton sounds as if it's worth a try." When I talked with other coordinator/trainers at conferences, they agreed that positive response, reflected both in students' comments and in a large number of volunteers, could mean that the *idea* of peer mediation was initially accepted by students as something valuable.

However, fifth-grade student Peg Maki's question, delivered as she stooped over the bubbler to get a drink, gave me reason to pause.

"Did I make it into *your club?*"

Selection Issues to Consider

I found myself thinking about Peg's perception each night during that week as I added the day's student and teacher results to the nomination grids (see Figure 5.4). Peg's question brought several issues to the forefront.

What happens when more students volunteer than are needed to start up a program? Any selection process affects *and rejects* students. As I pored over program materials (see Appendix A.2), it was difficult to locate detailed recommendations on selection issues.

In an article, Koch and Miller (1987) stated, "As part of the selection process, ask children to nominate peers; and encourage volunteers. Have all candidates fill out applications, which must also be signed by their parents and include a teacher recommendation. From the pool of nominees and volunteers, the teacher-coordinator can then choose a group that is representative of the school's ethnic, gender, and age mix" (p. 62).

Cohen (1987b) offered a list of "things to consider" when deciding which students will be trained:

> The training group should be diverse and represent a cross section of the school community (ethnic, racial, socioeconomic, academic, and personality diversity).
>
> To what extent will students with discipline problems and other "at-risk" students be targeted for training?
>
> Will an existing group be trained (i.e., student council, school safety club) or will a new group be created?
>
> Will only those recommended by faculty and/or administrators be considered for training? (p. 2)

Another suggestion came from Schrumpf, Crawford, and Usadel (1991): "In a school of 800 to 1000 students, it would be good to choose twenty-five to thirty students" (p. 23). Yet, there was nothing to clarify what made it "good" or how that ratio had been determined.

How is a decision made relative to the number of students that will be selected? I wished that I could train all sixty-two students who had nominated themselves. That would take separate two- or three-day trainings, and disrupt the school's schedule even more. Hampton's fourth- and fifth-grade teachers had already made a major commitment by releasing a small group of students from each of their classes for two days to train for a program that while full of promise, was unproven. My decision to choose twenty-five students was based on its being the average class size that I had managed as a former classroom teacher for years. I hoped that future selections and trainings would be supported by other teachers and staff who might become interested in joining me in an established program and perhaps enhance our ability to train every student who volunteered (see Chapter 10). But for the present, I was aiming to select approximately two dozen students from the sixty-two volunteers.

What process would work best to select a group of peer mediators? Peg's question made me appreciate how others could perceive of the peer mediation program as *my club*. Although I was working alone to implement it, I needed to be explicit about enlisting help during each phase. Cohen (1995) considered the time and effort involved and offered the "most efficient way to accomplish [selection of peer mediators]—and a way that includes staff in another element of the program—is to solicit recommendations from teachers and administrators . . . Some programs require that students receive two staff nominations to qualify for selection" (p. 117). However, I conceptualized the program as belonging primarily to students and supported by the coordinator/trainer, teachers, administrators, and parents. Thinking through the selection process, the model that made the most sense to me had five components and required input from several groups.

Student nominations support the rhetoric of peer mediation programs. To have a peer mediation program empowers students by giving them the opportunity to solve their own problems without the intervention of adults. Enlisting their help in selecting peer mediators engages them in the process by involving them in the decision-making process. If the message to students is "this is your program," then asking students to nominate others seems like a necessary component of the selection process.

Teacher nominations acknowledge their experiences with students. I included teachers' nominations during each class presentation (see Chapter 5) because their recommendations will be an important ingredient to fold into the mix of information about students who have volunteered. Not to ask for their input would alienate one of the most powerful and knowledgeable group of supporters.

Interviews with each volunteer give students an opportunity to respond to and ask questions. I designed a form with large spaces between each question to enable me to sit with students and take notes that I would refer to later (see Figure 5.3). My experience has been that interviews, although time-consuming (Cohen 1995, p. 118), are an essential piece of the selection process. An interview can be an intensely personal event, and you should be aware that students may open up and tell you more than you expect. Because I had taught conflict resolution lessons with the guidance counselor, Clare Riley (see Chapter 2), some students assumed that I was also qualified in that role. I was not, and when a student's talk moved into the territory of intrapersonal or interpersonal problems (troubles at home, for example), I explained the difference between my training and a guidance counselor's and offered to help him or her set up a time to talk with Clare.

You will gain insights about students' understanding of the process and the details of their commitment during an interview. For example, George Capshaw, a fifth-grade student who had almost daily conflicts with students and teachers, told me what helped him decide that he wanted to be a peer mediator. "I want to be like a guard and ask people a lot of questions. I want everyone to listen to me." I had the sense that he was interpreting the role in light of his own (lack of) self-esteem and saw it as an opportunity to hold a position of power *over* others.

I was surprised when several students warned me about others: "You know, Allison lies (or spreads rumors) about other people." I wondered about why some students felt they needed to say this to me until I thought about two mediator qualities I presented explicitly in the model: confidentiality (the ability to keep secrets); and honesty. Another student warned of an insecure classmate using the nomination process to test her popularity, "Elena volunteered just to see if she'll get picked, but then she's going to drop out." (She was selected and she did withdraw her name immediately, telling me, "I'm not ready for this yet.") When I asked fifth-grade teacher John Grayson why he thought students would bring up other students during *their interview,* he said, "Kids are realists. They think someone like that would spoil the program." It seemed to me that students were being morally scrutinized by their peers and teachers (Coles 1986) for a perceived lack of character.

More consistently, responses during interviews showed that students understood the model I presented in their classrooms (see Chapter 5). The volunteers wanted to "help people talk out their problems"; "help people stop fighting and be best friends again"; "help people solve problems and help myself because I have them, too"; "help my friends settle problems because they usually come to me anyhow."

Selection meetings form another important part of the selection process. Sadalla, Holmberg, and Halligan (1990) offered this suggestion: "In order that

---

Selection Meeting

Discussion Guidelines

What to consider when thinking about students who volunteered to become peer mediators:

Qualities:
- fair
- able to be neutral (not take sides)
- honest
- able to keep a secret (confidentiality)
- able to listen actively
- dependable and a hard worker
- willing to help others solve their own problems (not bossy)

The group needs to be balanced according to these specifications:
- gender
- race
- ethnicity
- negative and positive leaders*

*The category of negative leaders includes students who are "at risk," have below average academic standing, and/or may be perceived as "tough" or "bad." Positive leaders include students who are like the traditional good student, who does well academically and actively participates in the school's available leadership roles.

Figure 6.1   Selection Meeting

they have the respect and confidence of other students, Conflict Managers [peer mediators] are nominated by their peers although the final selection is reviewed by teachers" (p. II–12). I felt that I needed more input from teachers and administrators before the "final" selection. On the day that I completed the last classroom volunteering presentation, I put a list of all students who had volunteered in each Hampton teacher's and administrator's mailbox. At the bottom was the following message:

You are invited to attend the meeting to select
Hampton's first group of peer mediators
at 2:15 on Monday, January 11, in the office conference room.

That morning, I wrote a reminder in Hampton's daily announcements. At 2:15, seven classroom and two special needs teachers sat around a large table engaged in a discussion of how important it was that this group of peer mediators be representative of Hampton's population. We talked briefly about the factors of gender, ethnicity, and positive and negative leadership qualities (Figure 6.1). I pointed out that "academic standing generally has not been a criterion for selection" (Koch 1986, p. 28), but that I needed to know each student's standing generally so that the final list would not inadvertently consist of a preponderance of academically successful students.

Positive leadership seemed to be easily accepted as a criterion: students who were like the traditional "good student, who did well academically and actively participated in the school's available leadership roles" (Vermillion 1989, p. 15) would be considered as potentially strong peer mediators. The category of negative leadership provoked more discussion. It meant that "at-risk" students, possibly having below-average academic standing or perceived by students and teachers "as tough or bad," (p. 15) were to be considered as potential peer mediators. Koch and Miller (1987) advised:

> Select a group of student mediators to receive training from teacher-coordinators. *Those students selected need not be all the best nor model students.* Experience dictates that it is wise to choose a cross section, including some who are behavior problems. Ironically, but understandably these children often show major improvement in their new roles, as their needs for wholesome recognition are realized. One school reported that a "high risk street fighter" became an honor student. (p. 61)

The teachers gave an hour of their time to share their perceptions of the sixty-two volunteers on the list while I made notes next to each name. Salvatore was a below-average student academically who teachers had observed defusing fights on the playground. Carolyn had poor attendance and might miss her scheduled mediation duty or the after-school program. Alana seemed to be popular with her peers, but never finished her work and could turn out to be a quitter. Allison was a resource room student who worked well with her peers and had shown patience with others in some difficult situations. Zack was an outright bully and a manipulator who was not trusted to use this role to help others. When we ended the meeting, I thanked everyone for their input and said that I would be visiting the classrooms to read the final list in the morning.

A chart helps to organize factors for the final selection. (Figure 6.2). I had help from many people to bring me to the last phase of the selection process. The volunteers helped because their self-nominations made them eligible for selection. Information about the sixty-two volunteers came from notes taken during my interviews with them, nominations from their peers and teachers, and notes from the selection meeting.

Working that night to determine which students would emerge as strong candidates for training, I realized that each decision I made up to this point had an effect on what I was about to do. I glided the blue highlighter over volunteers' names on the class lists in order to see how many had nominated themselves from every fourth- and fifth-grade classroom. I decided to save these lists for September and promise first preference to any fourth-grade student who had volunteered, but was not selected this time. That week, I received a new middle school brochure that mentioned a peer mediation program starting up there in the fall, so I could offer that information to disappointed fifth-grade students. Next, I created the nomination grids for each classroom (see Figure 5.4).

I divided a large sheet of paper into eight boxes that I subdivided into "boys" and "girls," one for each classroom, because I wanted to make sure that there were gender-balanced peer mediators in every room. While there was a total of 83 boys and 67 girls in all the classes, and each class was balanced in proportion, I had a two-to-one ratio of girl to boy volunteers. That meant that if I decided

---

Selection Worksheet

Seeking access to your school's enrollment figures will help you get a sense of what you need to consider as you work to compose a group that reflects the student population. Check data with respect to grade level, gender, and ethnicity. Ask teachers to add input to the selection process.

Making an effort to consider factors of gender, grade level, ethnicity, perceived positive and negative leadership qualities, overall academic standing, student nominations, and teacher recommendations will be necessary to your selection process.

Name	Grade	Ethnicity	Perceived +/- Leader	Academic Standing	Nominations

---

Figure 6.2   Selection Worksheet

to create a fifty-fifty balance of girls and boys, it would favor the fewer boys who volunteered. Or I could maintain a larger number of girls because more had volunteered.

I noticed that in some rooms more than half the students had volunteered, while in others just a few had signed up. If I wanted to ensure that each room had some mediators, it would mean that those few had a better chance of being selected than did others who came from a class where there was a more enthusiastic response.

I pored over the nomination grids (see Figure 5.4) and penciled the names of volunteers from each room who received the largest number of nominations from peers and teachers, trying to weigh all the factors. I noticed that, for the most part, the teachers' nominations supported the students' choices. However, the list lacked the racial diversity of Hampton's population, which I had verified with the school's enrollment records. So, selection became a combination of those students with "most votes cast" and minority students who had fewer nominations, in order to reflect Hampton's student body. I noticed that whenever a student received a few in-class, out-of-class, and cross-grade nominations, they seemed to be based on three factors: ethnicity (Asians chose some Asians, Blacks chose some Blacks, Hispanics named some Hispanics), family ties (brothers, sisters, cousins nominating each other), and friendships (best friends nominating each other).

Other issues surfaced as I sat there generating a pile of pencil shavings and eraser crumbs. Political issues. Benjamin Pearson's name bobbed up among the fourth-grade list of volunteers, and I thought about the fact that his mother was president of the PTO—I had requested funds from them for peer mediators' tee shirts. Barbara Palimi's mother, who was herself a volunteer in Hampton's office, had stopped me as I walked by her desk and said, "You know, *my daughter* was picked as a peer mediator in her other school, but we moved here before she could be trained." Barbara had told me that in her interview, but her mother's reminder tolled in my memory when I saw her name. It would be unrealistic, as well as less than honest, to leave out the politics surrounding the selection process. I would not be the first, or last, program coordinator (or athletics coach) to come up against these issues during a process that necessarily eliminates students.

Late that night, thirty students' names remained on the list. Because it was a larger group than I had aimed for, I kept reconsidering each student and every factor. There were twelve boys and eighteen girls, approximately the same ratio of boy to girl volunteers (23:39), but not the same ratio of fourth- and fifth-grade boys to girls (83:67). Fifteen were White, eight were Hispanic, three were Asian American, two were African American, and two were biracial.

The process of selecting peer mediators is a delicate and complex task. There is no single best way to arrive at a list of names to announce or post on a bulletin board. These are some ideas that you might find useful to think about as you prepare for this phase of the program:

> Have I developed a list of criteria for selecting peer mediators?
> Have I gathered resource material that will help me (class lists, enrollment data)?
> Who will be asked to give input during the process and how will I encourage their participation?
> Have I developed a system for identifying potential peer mediators that reflects several perspectives?

A Step Back to Reflect

I visited each fourth- and fifth-grade classroom to announce the names of students who were to become Hampton's first peer mediators. I described the selection criteria again, as well as the process, in an effort to diminish the "my club" perception that Peg alerted me to earlier.

"Hampton's peer mediators will be a group made up of different kinds of students. Think about going to an assembly and seeing all fourth- and fifth-grade students sitting there together. You see girls and boys; some might be Irish American, Italian American, African American, Cambodian American, Korean American, or Puerto Rican—students who bring what they know about many cultures to Hampton. You see students who have different abilities—some are good in reading or sports or computers. Some are good at a lot of things, others are good at a few. There are some students everybody knows and others who are quieter and less well known. When I worked on the final selection last night, I had to think about including some of every kind of student to begin our program.

"I'd like to remind you that I had a lot of help in making up this list. Each of you nominated students whom you believed could be trusted if you decided to bring a conflict to mediation. I interviewed every student who volunteered and we talked about what it meant to become a peer mediator. I met with several teachers who talked with me about each volunteer. But it was still a difficult job in the end because there were sixty-two volunteers and this list has thirty names on it."

I paused to take in their expectant faces. The promise of mediation includes the phrase, "a win-win situation." This was not. "Before I read the list of names, I want to thank everyone who volunteered and ask, if you were not selected for this first group, that you think about a couple of things. First, your volunteering meant to me that you think mediation is worth using to solve conflicts. I hope you will bring your disputes to mediation. When you do, you will learn about mediation. That's the point, really—learning how to mediate comes from being a mediator *and a disputant*."

To each fourth-grade class, I offered, "If you volunteered this time and weren't selected, and you volunteer when you are in fifth grade, your name will go to the top of the list." To each fifth-grade class, I said, "The middle school is beginning a program in the fall, and I hope that you will consider volunteering there."

As I finished reading each list, some students looked disappointed and found it easier to begin searching in their desks for some lost object. Others approached me later in the hall or cafeteria and asked, "Can't you train two groups?" "What if Kelly drops out, can I take her place?" I explained that I could manage only one training that year, and if anyone dropped out, he or she could not be replaced. After school that day, a fourth-grade girl was seen sitting on her front steps, crying. When her neighbor, a newly selected peer mediator, asked her what was wrong, she sobbed, "I didn't get in."

I think about these students and offer this advice to coordinator/trainers who find themselves facing this difficult experience:

- Try not to forget how it feels to be rejected.
- Make yourself available to students in the cafeteria or on the playground, so that they can ask questions and say how they feel about not getting selected.
- Ask teachers to let you know about students who may not be taking their disappointment well and make an effort to talk with them.

A footnote in Richard Cohen's (1995) *Peer Mediation in Schools: Students Resolving Conflicts* advised, "Make sure you find a way to thank those students whom you do not select to be mediators so as not to alienate them from the program at this early stage." That seems like a good beginning, but does not address the importance of what it means to students when they do not hear or see their names on the final list. Expect their faces and voices to remain with you.

CHAPTER SEVEN

≈≈≈≈≈≈≈≈≈≈≈≈≈≈≈≈≈≈≈≈≈≈≈≈≈≈≈≈≈≈

Preparing Students to Mediate

Maybe Patrick Wasn't Exactly Neutral

At 8:00 A.M. on Thursday, January 14, twenty-eight students met me in the corridor outside Hampton's library to begin a two-day immersion in the role of peer mediator. The group had shrunk by two: one fifth-grade girl was unable to attend the weekly after-school training program, and a fourth-grade boy forgot his parental permission letter (see Appendix A.7) for the second day in a row.

I led two lines of students from A wing through the long white corridor connecting B wing to C wing. A few college students had begun to filter into the building for their 8:30 classes and cast surprised glances our way. I stopped the group outside the Professional Development Center. I had requested the use of this room weeks earlier because of its large size and location away from the hustle and bustle of the elementary school. I had spent an hour with custodians before school transforming it to accommodate these younger students.

"Before we go in, there's a coat rack in the far corner to hang your jackets. If you brought your lunch, put it on the rack underneath. Find the folder with your name on one of the chairs in the circle and sit down."

Alicia Hernandez, who was at the end of the line, observed when she passed me, "Did you notice that there's twice as many girls as boys?" I nodded.

Once everyone had settled in, we began by reading the chart paper with the first morning's agenda:

1. Names: Who Are We?
2. Break—snack and bathroom
3. Mediators: What We Say and Do
4. Small group/large group brainstorm

I looked around at the circle of expectant faces and felt a familiar first-day-of-school kind of knot in my stomach. "We'll start by doing activities designed to help us get to know each other better so that we can work together as mediators. Then we'll see if anybody can name everyone in the room." I noticed some students accepting the challenge immediately as their eyes moved from face to face around the circle. "After our break, we're going to look at the same four minutes of the video that I used during the classroom presentations (see Chapter 5) at least two more times. We'll try to figure out what Patrick and Rashad did and said during mediations that helped Nubian and Sarah to resolve their conflict. Studying them will help us to design parts of our program.

Before we go to lunch, we'll brainstorm a list of what we will have learned up to that point."

That morning, students began the process of adding a new Discourse to their repertoire, that of peer mediator. The following story illustrates how quickly these fourth- and fifth-grade students began to understand mediation process and their role in it.

After a discussion of how nonverbal behaviors ("tone of voice, facial expressions, gestures, eye contact, posture" [Sadalla, Holmberg, and Halligan 1990, pp. V–4]) could be perceived by others, we viewed the mock peer mediation video segment without sound (see Chapter 5). I had asked that students be ready to respond to the question, "What did you notice about the disputants' and mediators' body language?" We brainstormed a list of observations. "Nubian had an angry expression for almost the whole time, but Sarah had an innocent *I didn't do anything* look on her face." "Patrick looked at both disputants when he talked to them." "Rashad nodded his head when he understood something." "Both mediators looked serious and calm all the time." "Except for the time everyone signed the agreement, Rashad had to do all the writing."

Next, we looked at the video with the sound. "Be ready to talk about what you noticed this time."

T. J., an African-American student, had his hand up as soon as the handshakes ended the mock mediation on screen. "Neutral means you don't take sides, right?"

Murmurs affirming that definition rolled around the circle.

"Maybe Patrick wasn't exactly neutral."

"What makes you say that, T. J.?" I wondered out loud.

"Well, when Sarah said that she didn't mean to leave her out, Nubian said kind of sarcastically, 'Yeah, right.' Then Patrick goes, 'Shhhh!' But then when Sarah interrupts Nubian with, 'No, I didn't,' he didn't say anything to *her*."

"That's right!" "Yeah, I thought that, too," came from the circle.

T. J. offered an interpretation that opened a discussion of neutrality that would continue on and off until the final after-school session in June. He brought to light one of many dilemmas that could present itself during a mediation: a mediator asks that everyone agree to the ground rules (no interrupting), but the manner in which he or she holds disputants to them could be perceived by the disputant as being unfair, lacking neutrality, or in this case, even racist. Patrick's quick "Shhhh" tipped the scales for T. J.

Discussions were sustained, fast-paced, and complex. By the end of the morning, we lost a third volunteer. As we headed back toward the lunchroom, Scott Pierce, who, like T. J., was perceived by teachers as a "negative leader," blurted out, "This is too confusing. I don't want to do it." While the others lined up for lunch, I talked with him about his decision. He seemed firm about it, and so I said, "Since becoming a peer mediator is voluntary, I accept your decision, Scott. I hope if you have a conflict with someone in school, you'll choose mediation to help you solve it." He looked relieved and stepped into the lunch line.

Initial Training: What to Expect

While I write this chapter, I am simultaneously planning to train Hampton's fourth group of peer mediators. I perused my notes, materials, and plans from that first experience and asked myself what I had learned since then that could help you to plan your initial training and to know what you might expect.

Try not to get overwhelmed when you realize how much there is to accomplish during an initial training. While I was unable to locate much detailed information when I struggled with selection issues, it was quite the opposite when it came time to plan the initial training. There was a wide, even intimidating, array of material available (Schrumpf, Crawford, and Usadel 1991; Sadalla, Holmberg, and Halligan 1990; Meyer 1990; Dreyfuss, Carter, and Zimmer 1991; Johnson and Johnson 1991; Kreidler 1990). Typical advice begins:

> To conduct training most effectively, trainers will need to promote a climate that encourages participants to take risks, share, and become actively involved. The atmosphere must be cooperative and supportive; all students must be directly involved in the activities and practice the skills. (Schrumpf, Crawford, and Usadel 1991, p. 39)

The challenge lay in discovering for myself which activities fit Hampton's students, my objectives, and the two-day time frame.

At first, I bombarded myself with questions. Will the peer mediators understand the necessity of confidentiality, neutrality, and voluntariness? Will they recognize a power imbalance? Will the peer mediators know when and how to ask open-ended questions? How will they begin to tease out underlying issues? Will they recognize a fair and balanced agreement? At that point, it was useful for me to focus on the operative word—*initial.* I looked ahead. All peer mediation manuals mentioned "regular ongoing training" when you build on basic skills and strategies. The weekly after-school program was to begin the following Thursday.

Include "basic skills and strategies" for your initial training that are determined by the quality and quantity of experiences your students have had in conflict resolution and mediation. Besides being a former Hampton Campus School teacher, I had worked in classrooms on a regular basis the previous semester during Clare Riley's guidance activity periods. I also supervise elementary education interns and methods students at Hampton. This daily contact allows me to monitor what students might be learning about conflict resolution and affects plans for initial and ongoing trainings.

As you get to know your school (see Chapter 2), you may find that there is schoolwide involvement across the curriculum in conflict resolution which provides students with a substantial knowledge and experience base. However, it is best not to assume that a districtwide, *public* commitment to conflict resolution and peer mediation has filtered into every classroom. It is worth taking time to talk with teachers and students to discover what, if anything, students already know about conflict resolution and mediation, so that you can build on it. If the language of conflict resolution (I-messages, expressing emotions, identifying conflicts in varying contexts, active listening, creative problem solving) is already an established and explicit element in your school's culture, then an initial training can focus on enhancing students' third-party negotiating skills (Fisher, Ury, and Patton 1991; Ury 1991; Johnson and Johnson 1991). Ultimately, it will be up to you to assess your school's and community's familiarity with mediation concepts and to determine how that assessment will affect your initial training plans.

Negotiate with teachers and administrators the amount of time that can be devoted to initial training. Peer mediation manuals recommend a minimum of ten to twenty hours for an initial training, preferably uninterrupted over a period of two to four days. A program coordinator/trainer needs to keep in mind that this experience is a basic preparation to be followed by regular ongoing trainings, such as a weekly after-school program. However, it is important to consider your training time request from a teacher's point of view. A student's involvement during initial training will mean missed classes. Will class work be made up? Will homework be assigned from teachers? These are issues that need to be explored with teachers if you expect their support. It was my experience (and still is as I work with them in preparation for our fourth initial training) that Hampton teachers understood that their students would be involved in a positive, useful, *intense* learning experience that utilizes skills and strategies important to critical thinking and authentic problem solving. Many expressed a perception that certain students' gains in improved self-esteem was worth sacrificing two days of standard curriculum. The one teacher who initially required students to see him at the end of the day to pick up homework changed his mind when they arrived.

Determine the purposes and experiences basic to all initial trainings. Students need immersion in the roles of mediator *and* disputant from the start. Observing and participating in mediation role plays are a staple of adult and student mediation training. Many classroom teachers already appreciate the value of role play and its rich rewards of perspective taking and constructing knowledge (Finn 1993). Moreover, it is through the talk that follows each experience that students learn to make sense of it: "How did you feel when Joey said that to you?" "What did you think about when you were asked to tell your side of the conflict?"

Before I set the peer mediators into their first role plays, I used a portion of a video (Bankier and Dondlinger 1991) to help them begin to analyze the steps of the process and language ("Everything we say here is confidential." "What I heard you say . . .") I would also suggest seeking help from other peer mediation programs for role-play models to observe. Future groups were able to observe live role plays and critique them using a checklist (Figure 7.1) because second-year peer mediators volunteered to perform them.

Focus on enhancing students' self-esteem and connecting their sense of themselves to the role of peer mediator. Improving students' self-esteem is a purpose that supports common threads running through the fabric of a peer mediator's role—it might help to think about self-esteem and group identity as the warp and woof of the mediator's identity. When I recalled my own thirty-hour initial training, I noticed how many activities helped bolster my self-confidence and made me feel as if I were capable of assimilating at least some of what there was to learn. When I planned the initial training, I decided to use activities that focused on a basic self-esteem concept—names:

Checklist for Role Play Observer

Observer's Name _____

These are some things that I noticed and will tell mediator _____
more about *after* the role play is finished:

Body Language
____gestures   ____ facial expression
____eye contact   ____ posture
____seemed to be putting him/herself into each disputant's place in order to
understand what disputant said and felt

Language
____tone of voice   ____ used disputants' names
____sounded confident   ____ sounded respectful
____introduction   ____ restated disputants' words
____used neutral language,   ____ asked follow-up questions to get
did not offer advice or   needed information
suggestions   ____ summarized conflict
____reminded disputants of   ____ shared responsibilities with
rules   co-mediator
____agreement writing
____wrap up

1. I like the way_____
              (mediator's name) (did what?)

2. Comments and questions for _____
                          (mediator's name)

Figure 7.1   Checklist for Role Play Observer

Print the letters of your first and/or last name/s from top to bottom, instead of
across a paper. Using the first letter on each line, write words or phrases that
describe you or something you do well. Think about your strengths, the kinds
of things you have been proud of doing, words others have used to describe
you that have made you feel good, activities that you look forward to doing.
Be ready to share at least one with the group.

Tell a story about your name. What does it mean to you? What do you know
about how you were named? What do you like about your name?

It worked well to end these activities by talking about the following ideas:

How does it feel when someone uses your name with respect?
How does it feel when someone takes the trouble to learn your name?

Why does it become important for disputants to hear their names several times during a mediation?

Who can name everyone in our group?

Self-esteem can be the outcome of accepting and overcoming a challenge (Csikszentmihalyi 1990), such as becoming a mediator. More hard work lies ahead for the peer mediators, but I found that it is effective to have them reach into their memories and share past successes. One activity aimed at doing this begins with arranging students in two circles, one inside the other, facing each other. They have three minutes to tell their partner about one thing they were proud that they did; one thing that they learned that took hard work; a story that they would *like* to have people tell about them. The partner listens, then restates. The partner takes a turn during the next three minutes. After each round, the inner circle moves over one person to the left and repeats the pattern of telling, listening, and restating.

Each activity ends with "What do you think this activity has to do with mediation and with being a peer mediator?"

In spite of my belief that initial training was a gathering of people who cared about others, my experience as a classroom teacher taught me to expect to deal with interpersonal problems within the group. Coordinators and trainers strive to have individual students coalesce as a group, but teachers and administrators recognize the heavy baggage that may come with past relationships among students. It did not take long for that reality to be added into our first day together.

As the peer mediators lined up for dismissal, fifth-grade student Natalia Durgin stomped her way over to me to hand me a note that had been intercepted by a friend of hers. "What am I supposed to do with this?" The group's end-of-the-day chatter suddenly stopped. I read the torn piece of white-lined paper that said, "Dear Sandy, what are you going to do after school? That Natalia thinks she's so important because she uses big words. [signed] Lea." A small fourth-grade girl, Lea Rodriguez, would have withdrawn to the safety of her shell if she could have transformed herself into a turtle. I could read students' minds in the thin slice of silence I took to gather my thoughts. *What's she going to do now?* We had five minutes of travel time through two wings to meet the buses.

"Natalia, I can understand how this must upset you. Can you and everybody else wait for a discussion of this first thing tomorrow?" Everyone nodded. "Will this be one big group mediation?" came a question from the line. "Not unless they both agree to it," came an answer from someone who understood voluntariness.

As we gathered the next morning for our second day of training, Lea and Natalia planted themselves in front of me. Natalia said, "Things are okay between us now. We talked it over and Lea apologized to me." Lea nodded.

I said, "Thanks for telling me that you worked it out yourselves. I'd still like to talk this morning about mediators having disputes because I think it will help us learn more about our role." They both agreed.

"What happens when mediators have conflicts, especially with each other?" was the question when I opened the circle discussion.

Natalia said, "You will always have problems, and people will get angry with you. But it doesn't mean that you aren't a good mediator. I think that sometimes that's a good example—mediators aren't perfect."

Billy Glenn asked, "Doesn't it depend on how we solve the conflict?"

T. J. added, "Some people believe that mediators are supposed to be perfect angels. I don't want to act smart, but I'm not perfect."

Kristi said, "I think that you can say that we weren't trained *not to have conflicts.*" Her comment drew several pleased and amazed gasps.

Elizabeth clarified Kristi's idea for herself by stating, "We're trained to help solve conflicts, not to be immune."

As peer mediators talk their way to understanding their role, they are turning over various perspectives brought about by their awareness of social traditions. Their role is grounded in conflict. When that word is said in a group, smiles do not usually appear and eyes do not light up. Now you have a group of students who have decided to *become identified with the concept and who will work to reverse negative attitudes toward it.* A mediator embraces a powerful, socially constructed identity: to overpower violence and injustice with reasoned talk. Their most difficult challenge will be to defend themselves in light of how they will be understood and misunderstood by others.

Expect students to question and revise the language of mediation. We spent time talking about what we would say to disputants for our introduction because it sets the tone for the mediation process (Figure 7.2). I overheard T. J. reading it to his partner:

"Do you agree to no name-calling, put-downs, or physical fighting . . ." then he snorted, "*Physical* fighting? What *other* kind is there?"

I knew from Mr. Reynolds' Discipline Action Report that T. J. almost missed the training because of his suspension for hitting a White student who used a racial slur against him. I perched next to him and said, "Sometimes words can hurt as much as punches, T. J." He nodded.

There were differences in models when we were deciding on which exceptions to confidentiality to state ("Everything said here is confidential except for information about drugs, alcohol, or weapons on school property and abuse or suicide"). The last word provoked a thirty-minute discussion and derailed the agenda for the first of many times as students sorted through meanings.

"What if we say that and someone gets the idea from hearing it?" Alicia asked. "It will be our fault."

Another student responded, "My cousin killed himself and maybe if someone had talked to him about it, he wouldn't have. I really understand suicide." I include these children's comments because I believe that you need to be prepared for moments of moral reflection they are prone to share when they are given time and have occasion to talk about serious issues. At those points, you will need to stress the need to protect each other's privacy during discussions. I shared a saying I heard from another coordinator/trainer at a NAME workshop that students understood quickly: "What is said here, stays here. What is learned here, leaves here."

Address peer mediators' concerns. One of the most frequently asked questions during initial trainings has been, "What if disputants break out in a fight during a mediation?" It could happen, even though a cooling-off period between the conflict and a scheduled mediation is recommended. It is a concern that needs to be addressed. Peer mediators are doing a service for the school and need to feel safe while they are doing it. Hampton's peer mediators go on duty in the school's cafeteria *after* an adult volunteer or I arrive (for more details about supervision, see Chapter 10). I believe that school programs are obliged to have an adult within sight in the event that there is violence.

During the two days of initial training, we developed activities related to other issues of concern, including

- self-esteem and group identity
- recognition of the mediator's role
- development of an introduction
- skill in restating
- practice with the mediation sequence from referral to follow-up
- participation in role plays as a disputant and mediator

Were we able to complete everything? No. The second round of role plays, during which the mediators switched roles with disputants, was overruled by the clock. Some discussions could have gone on longer. Some should have been shorter.

Help prepare peer mediators to reenter the school's culture. When they leave the initial training each day, peer mediators will be asked questions about the mediation program. Sharing information about duty schedules, referrals, and follow-up interviews with them during the initial training will enable them to answer questions with confidence.

Another strategy to help peer mediators with the transition at the end of the day was the "What if . . ." box, which was filled with strips of paper. I had written situations that would lead to discussion because I wanted to prepare peer mediators to reenter what seemed like a faraway world outside the walls of the conference room. "What if someone asks you what you learned today?" "What if someone asks you a question about mediation and you aren't sure of what to say?" "What if someone teases you about being a peer mediator?" While several students responded, others listened and learned.

The following questions might help you prepare for training peer mediators:

Have I negotiated time and space with administrators and teachers for initial and ongoing training?

What can I realistically accomplish in the initial training?

What do I need to do to prepare for the initial training?

Have I assessed my needs for initial and ongoing training sessions (supplies, snacks, storage space)?

How can I access funds for tee shirts, hats, buttons, armbands?

Are there community resources that I can draw from to assist me in the training (coaches from a local community mediation program for role plays)?

Peer Mediators' Guide

As soon as you go on duty, both decide who will do which parts, how you will decide which disputant tells what happened first, and which mediator will record.

A. Introduction

Names!
    Introduce yourselves. Ask disputants to spell first and last names so recorder can write them on the report form.
Neutral!
    Explain you are neutral (won't take sides) and that you will not tell them how to solve their problem, but that *they* must think of ways to solve it.
Confidential!
    Explain that everything said is confidential (not repeated, kept secret) *except* for information about drugs, alcohol, or weapons on school property, and abuse or suicide.
Rules!
    Explain that there are four rules they will need to agree to:
- Try to solve the problem by coming up with solutions.
- No name-calling, put-downs, or physical fighting.
- No interrupting.
- Be as honest as possible.

Ask each disputant if he/she agrees to the rules and understands that mediation is voluntary. They or you can stop the mediation at any time.

B. What Happened (listening, restating, asking questions)

Who Goes First and Why!
    Mediator tells who will go first and why.
Telling What Happened!
    Ask each person what happened. Restate facts and feelings.
    "So, what you're saying is…"
    "So, you felt…"
    "Let me see if I understand what you just said…"
Needs!
    Ask each disputant, "What do you need to happen to solve this problem?"

C. Conflict Statement (restating and writing down)

Disputants Restate
    Ask each person to repeat what the other person said happened.
Mediators Summarize
    Summarize whole problem, including *key* facts and feelings that have been said by both.
Recorder Writes
    Recorder writes it on the report form under Conflict, then reads it back to disputants and asks them if it is correct. Make sure they agree that it is what they said.

Figure 7.2   Peer Mediators' Guide

D. Brainstorming Solutions (No agreements yet! We're just talking!)
Could! Could! Could! *You!* (Not the Other Disputant)
    Ask each disputant, "What *could you* do to solve this?"
    "What else?" "What else?" "What else?"
    (Remember: goal is for them to come up with as *many* ways as possible. If they get stuck, ask, "What would you tell someone else who had this problem to do?")

E. Resolutions (Are they fair, specific, balanced?)
Will! Will! Will!
    Ask each person, "What *will you* do now to solve this?"
    Restate. Record under Resolution.
Future! Future! Future!
    Ask each person, "What could you do differently in the future if the same problem arises?" Restate.

F. Wrap-Up
Ask the Problem Solvers to Spread the Good Word!
    To prevent rumors, ask the problem solvers to tell their friends that their conflict has been resolved.
Signatures!
    Have each person sign the report form with first and last names.
Congratulations!
    Congratulate them on working hard to solve the problem. Tell them that a peer mediator will meet with each problem solver in about a week to see how the situation is going. Shake hands with them and invite them to shake hands with each other.
After They Leave, Congratulate Yourselves on Your Hard Work!
    Seal the report form in an envelope and give it to the adult volunteer on duty with you.

Figure 7.2   (*continued*)

A Step Back to Reflect

Snow-day school cancellations forced us to reschedule the assembly/induction ceremony twice. As frustrating as it was for the mediators and me, it gave us additional time to use the first two after-school programs for rehearsing both role plays that were the teaching centerpieces of the assembly. The first role play was a property dispute—over a troll doll—which began when a promised lunchroom exchange of pizza for dessert was broken. The second role play involved a teasing/revenge dispute on the playground. With each rehearsal, mediators were internalizing the process, either by watching and giving feedback or by acting in the parts of disputant or mediator. The assembly/induction ceremony was establishing the peer mediation program's identity at Hampton, as well as providing an opportunity for all students to learn what to expect during a mediation.

    On the morning of February 1, twenty-seven peer mediators sat in a semicircle on the stage of Hampton's auditorium. A six-foot-long Hampton

Figure 7.3   Certificate of Mediation Training

Campus School Peer Mediation Program banner and a large, plain blue tee shirt were pinned on the curtain behind them. The lower section of the auditorium was filled with students, teachers, and support staff from classrooms scheduled for first and second lunch periods. The upper section was filled with some of the peer mediators' parents, pre-school siblings, grandparents, the assistant principal, and mediators from Riverton's community program.

Two peer mediators led the pledge of allegiance and I began, "Today is an historic moment . . ." During the role plays, I stood at the podium on the left of the stage and watched, a proud witness to these children's dedication and ability. It seemed to me that they were giving "the impression that their present poise and proficiency [were] something they always had and that they never had to fumble their ways through a learning period" (Goffman 1959, p. 47). I knew how hard they had worked to affect that demeanor. Lillian Comeau, the program's director, and Richard Camden, Hampton's principal, offered congratulatory remarks after the peer mediators received their certificates (Figure 7.3). I closed the assembly by thanking everyone by name, from the superintendent to the custodial staff. "And one last thing. Notice the plain blue tee shirts that the peer mediators are wearing. The PTO donated the money so that we could buy them. Now, Mrs. Demarco and I are working on a symbol contest that you will soon hear more about in your art class." Before the classes filed out of the auditorium, I invited the peer mediators and their families to share in the refreshments, provided by the principal, in the lobby immediately after the assembly.

The forty-five minute assembly/induction ceremony was filmed and edited to a half-hour program by the city's local access channel producer/camera technician, who was himself a longtime volunteer in Riverton's community mediation program. It was shown several times during the month.

At first and second lunch on the day of the assembly, Riverton's youngest mediators began their duties. I posted schedules in three places I knew students would have to pass each day: on a large bulletin board outside the library (I had requested it for mediation program use); in the corridor outside the restrooms; and in the cafeteria. The cafeteria supervisor agreed to let us store mediators' tee shirts and materials in a corner of the storage room.

Each first and second lunch period, two pairs of students went to the cafeteria storage room, picked up their mediation box and donned the large blue tee shirts that identified them as peer mediators. They set up their stations at two tables on the unoccupied side of the cafeteria, with clipboards holding agreement and follow-up forms (Figures 7.4, 7.5) and pencils ready to mediate students' disputes. There was a box of books to read if there were "no customers," which there weren't on that first day. Each day, two more pairs of peer mediators went on duty, walking around the playground with blue name tags that read "Hampton Campus School Peer Mediator" pinned to their coats.

I made another series of brief classroom visits after the February assembly, asking for questions from students and teachers. This time, I wheeled in an overhead projector and showed transparencies of the various papers that students would see peer mediators handling: the agreement and follow-up interview forms. Most of the teachers had posted envelopes of mediation request forms (Figure 7.6) in an easily accessible place, which I pointed out each time. I also told students that I would be keeping the original agreement form on file after making copies for each disputant and Mr. Reynolds. And I would mail disputants' copies home with a letter explaining mediation (Figure 7.7).

As program coordinator and researcher during the first several months of the peer mediation program, I was in the building Monday through Friday collecting mediation requests, screening disputes (Figure 7.8) and scheduling and supervising mediations within sight, not sound, of the mediators and disputants (Figure 7.9). By the time school reopened in September, several teachers and parents had joined me as adult volunteers in the lunchroom. See Chapter 11 for more details on peer helpers.

Peer Mediation Report Form

Peer mediators on duty: Disputants:

1. _____   1. _____
2. _____   2. _____
Date/s _____   3. _____

Place of conflict: ____ classroom   ____ hall   ____ cafeteria
                      ____ bathroom   ____ playground   other _____

Type of conflict: ____ arguing/fighting ____ teasing friendship
                      ____ rumor   ____ name-calling   ____ property
                      ____ threats   ____ broken promise other _____

Conflict: What happened? *Summarize* who said and did what. (Read this back to the disputants and make sure they agree to the facts.)

_____

_____

_____

_____

_____

Resolution: After thinking up several possible solutions, disputants pick the ones they will do.

_____ agrees to _____
_____
_____

_____ agrees to _____
_____
_____

_____ agrees to _____
_____
_____

_____ and _____ agree to _____
_____
_____

_____   _____
Problem Solver's Signature   Problem Solver's Signature

Figure 7.4   Peer Mediation Report Form

Peer Mediation Follow-Up Form

Case Number_____ Date _____
Peer mediator's name _____
Name of problem solver _____

1. Was a written agreement reached in mediation?
   _____ Yes   _____ No (If no, skip to #4)
2. If yes, how is the agreement holding up?
   _____ Everyone is keeping all terms of the agreement.
   _____ Everyone is keeping at least some terms of the agreement.
   _____ I am the only one doing what I said I would do.
   _____ The other person is doing what he or she said, but I am not.
   _____ No one is keeping any part of the agreement.
   What parts, if any, are not being kept? _____

3. Is the agreement working for you?
   _____ Yes   _____ No   _____ Somewhat
4. Was the mediation conducted fairly?
   _____ Yes
   _____ No, because _____
   _____ Somewhat, because _____
5. Do you feel that the original problem was settled?
   _____ Yes, because _____
   _____ No, because _____
   _____ Somewhat, because _____
6. Were you satisfied with your mediators?
   _____ Yes, because _____
   _____ No, because _____
   _____ Somewhat, because _____
7. Was the agreement fair?
   _____ Yes, because _____
   _____ No, because _____
8. Do you feel that your mediators took sides?
   _____ Yes, both did   _____ Yes, one did   _____ No, neither did
9. Would you recommend mediation to a friend who was having problems?
   _____ Yes, definitely
   _____ Yes, but only if _____
   _____ No
10. Do you think mediation made a difference in the way you and the other person get
    along? Are you getting along _____ better? _____ about the same? _____ worse?
11. Did you feel that the mediators took you seriously?
    _____ Yes, both did   _____ Yes, one did   _____ No, neither did
12. All in all, how successful do you think your mediation was?
    _____ Successful   _____ Partially successful   _____ Not successful
13. What did you like about mediation? _____

14. What did you not like about mediation? _____

15. Do you have any suggestions for making mediation more helpful? _____

Thank you for helping us with this follow-up.

Figure 7.5 Peer Mediation Follow-Up Form. (*Adapted from J. A. Lam. 1989.* School Mediation Program Evaluation Kit. *Amherst, MA: National Association for Mediation in Education, pp. 22–23.*)

Peer Mediation Request

Your Name _____ Date _____

People involved in the conflict	Homeroom Teacher	Agreed to mediate? haven't asked	Yes	No
_____	_____	____	____	____
_____	_____	____	____	____
_____	_____	____	____	____
_____	_____	____	____	____

What was the conflict about? _____

_____

_____

Figure 7.6   Peer Mediation Request

                                                    Date
Dear Parent or Guardian of _____

   Your child chose to resolve a problem in school by using peer mediation. When students are involved in a nonviolent conflict, they are given the option to resolve it by working with peer mediators who are trained to help them use talking and listening to work out solutions.

   Mediation is a process that helps students solve their own problems. It is voluntary and their discussion session is confidential. The enclosed agreement includes what the conflict was about and the resolutions that the problem solvers reached together.

   Our peer mediation program began in February 1993. I am attaching "Ten Reasons for Instituting a School-Based Mediation Program" by Albie Davis and Kit Porter; it tells about the benefits of this kind of conflict resolution program.

   If you have any questions or concerns, I hope you will call me (phone) or Mr. (   ), the assistant principal (phone).

                                          Yours truly,

_____   _____
Peer Mediation Program Coordinator   Assistant Principal

Figure 7.7   Letter to Disputant's Home

Screening Disputes

These are suggestions to help you know if a dispute is appropriate for peer mediation:

1. If physical violence (punching, hitting) has already been used, it is not appropriate.
2. After you ask "What's this about?" and in your judgment it is the type of conflict that children could resolve through talking it over with their peers, then it is appropriate.

    Typical disputes are about: name-calling, teasing, rumors, broken promises, friendship, property, threats.

    Make sure that all key people involved in this dispute are present.
3. You can give disputants these choices:

    a. talk it out between themselves

    b. ask for help to settle it:

    teacher

    the principal or assistant principal

    the guidance counselor

    peer mediators on duty
4. If *each* disputant chooses peer mediation voluntarily, then send them to the peer mediators on duty or fill in a request form and return it to the second-floor mediation mailbox.

Figure 7.8   Screening Disputes

Adult Volunteer Log

Please leave this schedule on the volunteers' clipboard and update it each time there is a mediation, peer helper session or a follow-up. Code mediations M-# and peer helper PH-#.

First Lunch 10:45–11:15

Case # and Date: Students' names   Completed follow-up

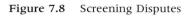

Second Lunch 11:15–11:45

Case # and Date: Students' names   Completed follow-up

Please write only names and dates on this sheet. Any comments or questions should be written on separate paper and left in my mailbox. Thank you. Page ———

Figure 7.9   Adult Volunteer Log

CHAPTER EIGHT

≈ ≈

Taking Hold

Hey, You Need a Mediation!

During those first few months of Hampton Campus School's peer mediation program, I felt a little like a neophyte gardener who had planted seeds and was wearing a path to the backyard checking the soil for the tiniest green sprout. I wondered if the program would take hold and be accepted by students in much the same way I had wondered if any students would volunteer to become peer mediators (see Chapter 5). I needed to watch closely, listen carefully, and above all, try to put myself in students' shoes and ask, "What does it mean to have a peer mediation program in my school?"

Gradually, the first signs of life appeared as students began to teach me how they were making sense of the program. One way was through their language play. In February and March, I circulated among the fourth- and fifth-grade lunch tables while the peer mediators were on duty. A typical interaction would look and sound like this: Jared catches my eye and pulls the fake punch aimed at François' arm. Feigning horror and looking sideways at me, François cries out, "We need a mediation!" It was a theme for which students created a number of variations as they interacted with me in classrooms, corridors, and on the playground. I would laugh and say, "That's right—words, not punches" and move on. However, their joke making told me that mediation Discourse had begun to be assimilated into the school's culture.

On April 13, I observed an example of the power of its language. At the end of recess, students flowed from all directions on the playground to form two lines on the sidewalk that runs along the edge of the building. As play areas emptied, I noticed a small knot of boys conspicuously rooted to their spots near the swing set, about five yards from where students were lining up. Even though I was at the far end of the playground, their body language was easy to read: fight about to begin. Three boys formed a semicircle around two red-faced opponents who were toe-to-toe with fists poised. Eighty students fell silent and watched as a teacher headed toward the warring parties.

Suddenly, Francesca Santana, a fifth-grade student whose voice had a natural chuckle trapped inside, called out from her place in line, "Hey, you need a mediation!" Laughter broke out everywhere. "Not mean or rude laughter," as Francesca would later describe it. Just laughter. The two boys relaxed their arms, looked relieved, and added their somewhat nervous laughter to the group's. In seconds, *one student's astute use of the word, mediation,* allowed them to save face and diffused the potential fight. They parted and walked into line.

I did not discover the nature of the problem or if the dispute was finally resolved, but the incident taught me how a single new word used by a student carried meaning sufficient to prevent physical violence, at least for the moment. Francesca, the expert language user, knew when and how to use the word in the context of a violent situation and relied on her humorous tone and inflection to carry her message (*"Chill."*). That her meaning and intent were shared by the group was illustrated by the behavior of over eighty students on the playground who understood and laughed with her and the disputants. The budding program had pushed its way into the sunlight of Hampton's playground.

I have since replayed that scene in my mind and wondered, What if Francesca had been a peer mediator (she had volunteered, but was not selected) and said those words in exactly the same manner? Would students have assumed that her new role inspired her to intercede? What would their reaction have been then? What if a teacher had said those words (with or without the humor)? How would it have been received by students? These questions helped me to consider the interaction from several perspectives and to better understand the meanings that seemed to be building around the peer mediation program.

Supporting Students' Curiosity About Mediation

It is especially important during the early months of a peer mediation program to give students opportunities to find out more about the mediation process and your program. Three days after the program started, Wanda Alamieda, a fourth-grade student who was noted for her antisocial behavior, asked me at the end of lunch, "Can we go ask mediators questions if there are no mediations?" I said that I would check with them at the next after-school program and let her know.

During the fourth-grade mediation duty the next day, Richard Walker and Crystal Andrews spread their clipboards and box of chapter books on the table. Crystal asked, "Any mediations today?"

"No, but . . ." When I told them about Wanda's idea, they seemed eager to use their duty to share what they had learned about mediation. Richard thought for a moment, fixed his shifting eyeglasses to their proper place on his face with an expert flick of his finger and said, "Sure, I think it's a good idea. But why don't we have a sign to let people know we will answer their questions? This way, people will know they're not here with a problem."

Richard's comment brought to mind Erving Goffman (1959, 1967), whose theories and research focused on how people behave in social situations, as well as the ways those behaviors appear to others. Here was a nine-year-old showing sensitivity toward the students' need to clarify their presence at the mediation area so that it would not be misinterpreted by others ("I'm just curious, not having a conflict"). He seemed to be aware of the need to communicate explicitly to students and teachers on the far side of the cafeteria that a situation different from mediation was taking place in the "front region," (the lunch tables on the unoccupied side of the cafeteria) which Goffman (1959) defined as "the place where the performance [the mediation] is given" (p. 107). That afternoon, I made and laminated a large folding sign that when dropped over the end of the table read: Mediation in Progress, and when reversed read: Open for Questions.

For the next several months, a regular stream of curious students sat with mediators and asked about the process and the new program. Open for Questions satisfied a need. As fifth-grade student T. J. Jackson put it during one after-school program discussion, "Some students are not used to the concept." By the end of June, students posed dozens of questions and participated in an added ritual that served to inform students about the program. It was a student-inspired method that educated others and also gave mediators an opportunity to verbalize their growing understandings of mediation.

I asked students' permission to join them during the first week of Open for Questions because I was interested in adding what I learned to my research data. I reasoned that it was appropriate because this interaction was not confidential, as mediations are. Each time I asked, students agreed to let me sit in. However, their nonverbal language told me that they seemed to be aware of my presence while I sat there. It made me realize that if I were a nine-year-old, it might have been very difficult for me to say no to a request from the program coordinator. I also noticed that the peer mediators seemed to rely on my giving them support when they answered questions, which I was all too ready to do, until I realized that there was something more important at stake: allowing time and space for students to teach each other what they knew about a new role without the presence of an adult.

My decision was to withdraw and observe them from the other side of the cafeteria while I circulated among the lunch tables. Occasionally mediators would come after me to get clarification on an answer. From a distance, I saw students teaching each other about the program. Their body language communicated a professional demeanor made explicit by their learned Discourse roles: serious expressions, occasional nods and smiles, the use of clipboards as props to show curious students the mediation guide, report forms, and follow-up questionnaires (see Figures 7.2, 7.4, 7.5).

During the second week of Open for Questions, Jasmine Rodriguez, one of the few peer mediators who had asked explicit questions about my role as researcher, came over to me before she started and said, "Shouldn't we be writing these down so you'll know what they're asking?" From that day, mediators wrote the questions on scrap paper and gave them to me at the end of their duty. Students' questions were about mediators feeling "scared" or "nervous" during training and mediations, and if mediators would get "kicked off" if they "got in trouble" or "got bad grades," or what would happen if mediators "messed up and took someone's side." One asked if mediators had to "take tests" or have "mediator homework." Many asked what mediators did during the after-school program. Students wondered about mediators becoming "scared when a friend asks for mediation" or, on the other hand, "when you have to work with someone you don't know." Others asked if mediators ever went to mediation themselves. They asked what would happen if mediators "forgot what to do." They were curious about what it was like to "work for Ms. Ferrara" (!) and asked, "Will she be here next year?" and "Do you want to be an adult mediator when you grow up, too?" One student wanted to know: "Do they pay you?" while others asked, "Why do you want to help people?" and "Do you feel special?"

Some wondered if there "was ever any violence during a mediation," and if disputants were "forced to come." One student asked, "How do you feel when you have three disputants and only two talk?" "What do mediators do when one person wants to solve the problem, but the other one doesn't?" Several asked, "How do you feel when people tease you about being a mediator?" and "What is it like when you get kids who won't listen to you?"

Students' ability to formulate questions for Open for Questions showed as much about what they knew and felt as what they did not know about mediation. Their curiosity taught me that they understood how difficult a task the mediators had undertaken. Students' questions alerted me to anxieties that they felt with respect to learning something new or their fear of violence erupting during mediations.

Program coordinators need to plan time to listen to peer mediators' perceptions of how the program is being received in the school's culture. Program descriptions suggest bi-weekly or monthly meetings to engage mediators in ongoing training activities and in debriefing discussions. Based on my experience, *weekly* meetings work best to provide an open forum for peer mediators to exchange ideas and extend their training. These frequent meetings allow peer mediators to teach you the meanings that are taking shape for them in and around the process and the roles they have acquired.

The setting for the centerpiece of our learning was the college classroom that I reserved for Thursday's after-school program. It was bleak and unadorned compared to the mediators' own classrooms. Instead of eye-catching posters and bulletin boards lining the walls and desks or tables spilling over with books and papers, we worked surrounded by bare white cinder block walls, chalkboards, and empty bulletin boards.

Minutes before each hour-and-a-half session was to begin, I shoved red, yellow, and blue metal tablet chairs into a circle, replacing the professor's neat, lecture-ready rows. Every Thursday, as the ear-splitting 2:00 dismissal bells finished ringing, the peer mediators and I met outside the elementary school library and walked through the connecting corridor toward the normally off-limits C wing. The mediators vied for first place in line so that the classroom lights, tripped by motion detectors, would come on when they entered the room. They threw their coats and backpacks against one wall, eyed our soda and cookie snacks on the green metal teacher's desk, and read the agenda that I had written on the chalkboard. A typical agenda would be headed by the date and look as follows:

1. journal entry
2. role play
3. snack
4. issues and concerns

I found it useful to start each after-school program by having them write a ten-minute journal entry that I would respond to and return at the beginning of the next session. Students wrote about mediation issues, as well as personal issues. During the implementation stage, I believed that it was crucial to establish a rapport with individual students, as well as to develop group identity. A dialogue journal helps establish and maintain that relationship.

Between February and June, there were seventeen after-school sessions. That portion of time devoted to "issues and concerns" gradually pushed its way to the top of the agenda. A mediator would raise a hand after finishing the journal entry and request, "Could I just say something about what happened today?" My response began with pointing out the importance to maintain confidentiality: "Certainly. But remember, we promised that 'everything said during a mediation is confidential,' so we need to be careful about how we talk about our concerns. For example, I might say, 'During a mediation about name-calling, when one disputant told his side of the conflict, he said the insulting name and made the other disputant angry all over again.' What do you notice about how I started to describe my concern?"

Natalia said, "You didn't use names. You called them disputants."

T. J. added, "The rest of us don't know what the insult actually was. It's like you're telling just enough to let us know what you're concerned about, so we can talk about how you handled it."

Once the peer mediators learned the pattern for talk, they began an out-pouring of talk that went on sometimes for forty-five minutes. There were days when I was discouraged by how little the peer mediators talked about the positive side of the job for which they had volunteered. I also felt the pressure to spend time in ongoing training activities, such as presenting role plays or evaluating the language of agreements. However, sessions were replete with talk about the problems they were encountering. In January, these volunteers declared that they wanted to help students solve their own problems. At first, I worried that the mediators were becoming discouraged. It took time to adjust *my agenda* and realize how much learning was occurring as they talked. It is through talk that complex and strategic meanings were reflected upon and reshaped, reformed and abandoned, considered and reconsidered. The more they talked about their issues and concerns, the more they learned, in the sense that Gee (1990) described:

> This teaching or reflection involves explanation and analysis, that is, breaking down the thing to be learned into its analytic parts. It inherently involves attaining, along with the matter of being taught, some degree of meta-knowledge about the matter. (p. 146)

Their authentic, practical problem finding, coupled with trial and error problem solving became the center of their learning experience, as well as mine.

An issue that emerged in the early weeks of the program again focused on students' curiosity about what it felt like to be "in a mediation" and the lengths they went to find out. In March, Elaine Lindquist wrote to me in her journal about an incident that happened on the playground:

> Two of my friends played a trick on me. They pretended to have a fight, so I mediated them. After I did it, they said that they made it up to see if I was neutral. But they did say that I didn't take sides, so it was good!

Elaine's entry showed me three things: first, she was feeling confident enough to use the process outside of her "scheduled mediation duty"; second, her friends were testing one of her qualities (neutrality); third, Elaine's friends "made [the conflict] up." This was supported by something I had learned. I told the mediators about a teacher who stopped me in the cafeteria and said, "I overheard some students saying that yesterday's conflict was made up." I shared

my response to her with the mediators: "While we want students to take mediation seriously, I think it's a good sign because it shows that they want to learn
about it."

Other peer mediators expressed concern about having "fake mediations."
When I asked them how they knew they were fake, they drew on evidence less
apparent than Elaine's: "The disputants were just too nice to each other." "I could
just feel it." I nudged, "What do you think that means?" They decided that some
students' curiosity was not being satisfied through Open for Questions.

"What can we do about it?"

Elaine's eyes lit up. "We used role plays in our training. What if they could
make up conflicts and do role plays with mediators if there were no real mediations scheduled? It would give us practice."

"If you will be using an agreement form, it might confuse me when I collect
the papers at the end of lunch."

"We can write 'role play' at the top."

Richard, ever-sensitive to how students involved in role plays might be
perceived by others, added, "And everyone will know it's not a mediation because
we won't turn the sign around."

The next day, no "real" mediation referrals were left in our mailbox. I stood
at the end of each lunch table flanked by groups of students eating their lunches:

"Remember when the mediators did the two role plays at the assembly?
They were wondering if any of you would like to make up conflicts and do role
plays with them if there are no mediations scheduled."

The pile of blue agreement forms marked "role (or roll, row, roe) play"
grew over the weeks as students made up interpersonal conflicts that seemed to
mirror authentic ones they had observed, participated in, or heard about in the
community:

> Carol claims that Candi threatened to beat her up. And she feels mad and
> upset. Candi claims that Carol's gang threatened to beat her up because
> she would not join her gang and she feels mad and upset.

> Jake was the pitcher and Kolby kicked the ball. It hit Jake in the face and
> he chased Kolby. They are both mad at each other.

> Ann put milk on Jenn's hair. Ann called Jenn a name. Both of them are
> mad at each other.

The need for Open for Questions and role plays diminished after the first
several months of implementation. While both ideas worked to educate students
during those days when it *was a new concept*, peer mediators began to complain
during the after-school program that students were "coming up to ask silly
questions, like 'Do you know how to milk a cow?'" Although the mediators
decided to keep it as an option, they added the proviso: "Only if they're serious"
and retained the right to ask students to go back to their lunch table. The
following year, it became less expected (and necessary) as a part of their duty.

Creating Opportunities to Teach Others About Mediation

In-school publicity was a matter of thinking about paths to students' consciousness as they moved through a typical school day. One of the first things you
notice when entering Hampton's main door is a large bulletin board. Teachers

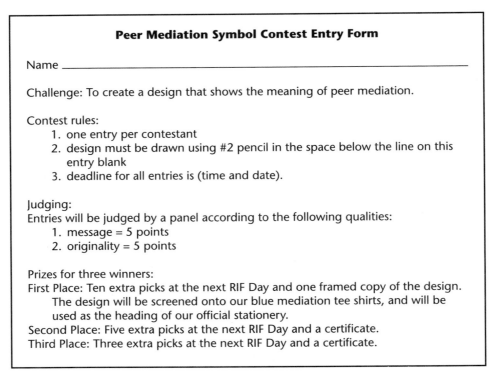

Figure 8.1   Peer Mediation Symbol Contest Entry Form

volunteer to decorate it each month. Students pass it each day on their way to the cafeteria. I asked the principal and the teacher in charge of coordinating its use for the opportunity to declare in large letters: March Is Mediation Month! Meet Your Peer Mediators. Each mediator, photographed wearing a plain blue tee shirt, smiled back at observers. Since that year, March *is* Mediation Month at Hampton because the bulletin board has become a program tradition.

Because the mediators' tee shirts were undecorated, they were an inviting canvas for an April symbol contest to publicize the new program. It was an opportunity for me to learn more about the meanings students were constructing through symbol making. Lauren Demarco, the art teacher, planned two lessons for each class from first and second lunch and I devised an entry form (Figure 8.1). We talked about her perceptions of the students and their responses:

> It was a pleasure seeing their enthusiasm. They came in with prior knowl-edge from your presentations and that was a help because it saved me from explaining peer mediation. My job as an artist was to help them transcribe all that knowledge into a simple symbolic image.
>
> There were three categories the students drew from. The most common were the peace symbol, the two finger peace sign, and the lion [Hampton's mascot]. One of the most original was the Band-Aid. No one else did that. I wondered if François' perception was a masking over of the problem rather than a solution. Then there was the clipboard and people sitting at tables. All these are things I didn't talk about with them [Figure 8.2].

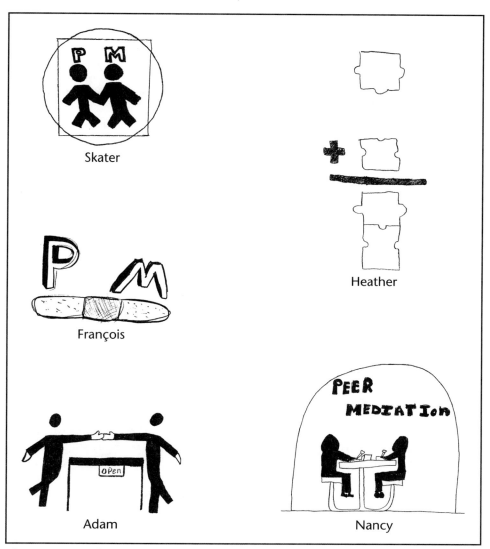

Figure 8.2   Student Symbols for Peer Mediation

I think their perception of the peer mediation program is a positive one because I would have gotten, "Do I *have to do this?*" Their emotions come out readily. They were very enthusiastic.

During a later conversation with François, I asked, "If someone wondered what a Band-Aid had to do with mediation, what would you say?" He responded immediately with, "It's about healing." These two brief exchanges added to my understanding of symbol making by reminding me that there would be differences between students' and teachers' interpretations of the new mediation program ("masking" or "healing"). The symbol contest was an occasion for students to construct meanings, for others to interpret their meanings, and for me to learn different perspectives.

Symbol contest prizes included a framed copy of the design and extra selections at the school's upcoming Reading Is Fundamental book giveaway. The twenty-two finalists' designs hung for a month in the corridor leading to the cafeteria. Creating opportunities to raise students' consciousness about mediation should be a relatively simple in a school's culture where essay, poetry, and art contests are at home and bulletin boards and wall space provide fertile ground for message-sending.

The challenge of educating the community about peer mediation falls to program coordinator/mediators who need to be sensitive to and informed about the ways in which mediation supports or conflicts with established patterns of dispute resolution. Because program coordinators become liaisons to administrators, parents, and the community, their skills in educating others about mediation are crucial to a program's success. In her study of an urban middle school peer mediation program, Ellsworth (1993) found that "even if all the staff had been handpicked and had had extensive training, the lack of community understanding, use and support of problem solving conflict resolution would have made program implementation difficult" (p. 197). If parents are expected to support peer mediation programs and encourage students to consider using the process when an appropriate conflict arises, then they need to understand mediation (see Chapter 5).

In order to bring news of your peer mediation program outside the school's walls, you will need to tap community connections. Riverton's local access channel regularly featured a school-oriented panel discussion show, which was produced by the same mediator who filmed our induction ceremony (see Chapter 7) and was hosted by a Hampton teacher's father.

It took several phone calls to arrange for an appearance on "School Scenes." I asked for volunteers from among the peer mediators and we picked their names out of a hat. One icy night in March, they, their parents, and I crowded into the studio waiting room. Show host Bill Green was to interview me and three peer mediators in each of two segments. When it came time to begin, I asked the three peer mediators sitting near the door to be in the first segment. We went down to the studio, filmed the segment and switched to the second group at the halfway point. I must note here the skill with which these nine- and ten-year-old children fielded Bill's questions about what it was like to mediate a dispute and what they had learned in their new role. We witnessed their initial nervousness subside and confidence take its place.

In the rosy glow of praise that followed the first airing of the show, a Hampton teacher stopped me in the hall and asked, "Did you notice that you had the three non-Whites in one group and the three Whites in the other?" I had to admit that I had not noticed and explained my spur-of-the-moment selection process. The question taught me another lesson about people's perceptions and the time I should have taken to think through details (such as how seating could be interpreted).

A plan to publicize Hampton's peer mediation program on the regional commercial network news station was less successful, in spite of their ongoing "Stop the Violence" campaign. My offer to have them interview students and film a role play was met with "A role play? Sorry, we're into reality." They wanted to be able to film an actual mediation. Fitting into their "reality" would mean compromising our promise of confidentiality to disputing students.

Contacting Riverton's two newspapers was another step in publicizing the peer mediation program. The *Sentry* is small and local, and the *Clarion* is large and regional with a north county insert devoted to Riverton and Lincoln. In March, I called both newspapers and described our new program. The *Sentry*'s assistant city editor interviewed me in my office and then came to the cafeteria to interview students and peer mediators. The article was accurate and clearly written, two qualities I grew to appreciate when I had the next experience.

The *Clarion* sent Michael Larson, who began by telling me about his last job, that of investigative reporter in Washington, D.C. He insisted that I show him any agreements that had been reached. When I repeated the principle of confidentiality, he said, "That's okay, I'll just blacken the names out." He did not get to see the agreements.

"Well then, can I see a mediation?" I told him that there were none scheduled for that day. "Since mediations are confidential, you would not be able to sit in. But you could watch a role play." He turned down the role-play offer and continued the interview in the cafeteria.

Larson and I circulated among the tables, and he asked students, "What do you think of your peer mediation program?" I brought him to the peer mediators' tables. "What do you say when feuding students first sit down?" Kelly Felenzo said, "Well, one of the first things we tell them is that we are neutral, which means we don't take sides . . ." The next day, Larson's piece appeared with a description of peer mediation that included a disputant taking a conflict "to court," where two mediators in blue tee shirts—"junior Judge Wapners"—sat filling out forms and asking "standardized questions, all for the purpose of getting at the matter." Kelly's explanation of neutrality was lost on him, as well as other key concepts I had tried to explain.

Like a gardener, a program coordinator needs to prepare the soil (teach and seek volunteers), do the planting (train), and tend the seedlings (schedule mediations and plan ongoing trainings). You will need to watch and listen and learn to read the signs that direct you to clip here or sink a stake there and be prepared when an unexpected sprout appears. It is the experience of moving between action and reflection that permits response to your program's growing and changing needs.

The following questions may be helpful in monitoring daily observations and interactions during the early stages of program implementation:

> As I observe student-student interactions during the school day, is there verbal or nonverbal evidence that points to an integration of mediation theory or practice into the context of their lives?
>
> How can teachers, staff, parents, and administrators help me to learn more about students' response to the new peer mediation program?
>
> How can I utilize the community's resources and personnel to help me publicize the program?
>
> How can I tap local media support during the implementation stage?

A Step Back to Reflect

Evidence of successful peer mediation programs is often based on figures that show lowered rates of office discipline referrals and suspensions or physical violence (Lam 1989a, 1989b). While program evaluations are frequently based on such quantitative data, results may not become apparent immediately. In other words, you may find that students are choosing mediation to settle disputes, but there is little change in the number of feuds that find their way to the administrator in charge of discipline. According to Cohen (1987a), this is a typical response to a new program: "At the conclusion of their first year the coordinators will likely find that their program statistics lack the sort of undeniable glow necessary to convince skeptical administrators" (p. 3). However, a change came about in the following school year. In an October 1993 interview, Jim Reynolds said,

> Things are quieter this year and I would think that mediation is part of it. In fact, so far this year, I have had zero social conflicts [such as], "She said this about me." No name-calling, no teasing this year at all. On any given week, I would get four, five, six of those and I get zero. That is a tremendous savings of time for me. I think the kids are used to knowing what could go to mediation because what I get is physical [fighting], a lack of respect for adults—that's what I deal with. Students know what the separation is . . . I think that they know more how to solve their problems or where they can go to solve their problems. I know that more people have come into the building [this year] and have noticed a definite difference in attitude.

When I later compared Jim Reynolds' Pro-Social Discipline Action Reports with the same time period the previous year (September through February), the number of discipline reports from the assistant principal that were returned to teachers and mailed home to disputants' parents dropped from two hundred to one hundred. The presence of a peer mediation program may be one of many factors that produced what some might point to as "improved school climate."

By the last day of school on June 17, thirty-eight disputing students and eight teachers wrote forty-six requests (see Figure 7.6) and left them in the mediation mailbox that was attached to our bulletin board in the corridor. Disputants worked their way to thirty-three agreements. Conflicts developed over harassment: name-calling (13), teasing (14); relationships: broken promise (1), friendship (4), boyfriend/girlfriend (3); property (5); rumors (4); and threats (2).

Throughout this chapter, I stressed the importance of paying careful attention to the signals students were sending about their understanding of the peer mediation program. But underneath the surface of students' acceptance, a form of blight was growing in its tissues. It is a story that begins with a statistic: between February 1 and May 21, there was an average of one mediation every two and a half days. Between May 24 and June 17, mediation referrals increased to more than one a day. What caused that figure to rise? It was related to one factor—the letter home.

SECTION THREE

≈≈≈≈≈≈≈≈≈≈≈≈≈≈≈≈≈≈≈≈≈

Maintaining a Peer Mediation Program

CHAPTER NINE

≈ ≈

The Letter Home

Why Do They Need to Know?

Think back to Danny Rodriguez and Jamie Caron as they sat in Mr. Reynolds' office watching him type their Pro-Social Action Report into his computer (Chapter 1). Their situation meant "double trouble" for them: first, they were sent to the assistant principal's office for fighting in class and would face the consequence of losing recess that day; second, copies of the report that would be mailed in unmarked envelopes to their homes might result in another set of consequences. I arrived the hard way at the crossroad of understanding what "double trouble" meant to students, because Danny and Jamie were bound up in a dilemma that related to Hampton's peer mediation program, and that only became clear once the program had been implemented.

Mediators promise disputants during the introduction that "everything *said* here is confidential." The written agreement is a private document usually held by the disputing parties and the program coordinator. In some schools, the original written agreement is filed by the program coordinator, with no copies distributed to disputants. I felt that it was important for students to receive a copy of the agreement in order to verify the importance of their having solved the problem, as well as to remind them that they needed to keep their part of the agreement. Because the agreement was given to me at the end of the mediation, I needed time to make copies. Rather than locate and interrupt students in class, I decided that I would mail copies home. I assumed that the strength of Hampton's program would come from two features: the peer aspect ("kids helping kids," with no adults involved during the mediation); and the fact that solutions to the conflict would come only from disputing students themselves, as opposed to arbitrators or judges (in this case, Mr. Reynolds). Hampton's peer mediation program, with its confidential talk and letter sent home accompanying the agreement (see Figure 7.7), seemed to be an extension of the existing pro-social approach to solving conflicts, which advised parents of their children's actions as problem solvers (see Chapter 1).

My assumptions may have been correct when viewed from an adult's point of view, but they were off the mark from many students' perspectives. If I had viewed the culture of the school and neighborhood *with students' eyes* when I began the program, this chapter would have had a different focus. The story of "The Letter Home" begins in February and ends in June, the first five months of the program. It had serious implications that stemmed from issues of disclosure and maintaining confidentiality. I believe that it is important to share because it could help adults understand the need to pay close attention to verbal and nonverbal signals that students send.

Daily mediation duty meant a stop at the mediation mailbox to check for requests. One morning in March, I reached in and found one describing a conflict over name-calling that was written by Juan Mendez, one of the two disputants. When I arrived in the cafeteria, I found Juan standing in the lunch line, drew him aside, and said, "I have your request for a mediation between you and James. First, I have to ask you: Are you doing this voluntarily?"

"Yes, I am. I've been to mediation before with another problem. And so has James."

"I don't see him here. I have to ask him the same thing. Where is he?"

"I think he's upstairs in our classroom working."

Juan and I left the cafeteria. Because of this delay, I knew that if James agreed to the mediation, it would have to be scheduled for the next day. When we arrived at their fifth-grade classroom, we saw James working with a few other students and their teacher, Ms. Vincenzo. When she looked up, I caught her eye and pointed to James. He had already seen Juan and me and was walking toward the doorway. By the time he reached us, he was crying. We stepped out into the deserted corridor.

"James, why are you upset?"

"Because when I went to mediation last week, you sent the letter home, and my father hollered at me."

I found it difficult not to be devastated by this student's tears and explanation. I quickly offered to call his father and explain how mediation was different from being disciplined by Mr. Reynolds.

"No, don't do that," he said to the floor as he composed himself.

"I could write a note at the bottom of the letter saying that we are proud of you for choosing mediation to solve a conflict and that parents need to show support when you use the process." The words that I reached for came directly from my own mediation coordinator Discourse, but they felt hollow in this situation. James looked up, thought a few seconds, and nodded.

"You know that unless you both agree to mediate this dispute, you will not have to go to mediation." I waited for their decision.

"I still want to do it," Juan said and looked over at James.

"I'll do it." His look and tone of voice told me that he had made the decision voluntarily, although he might find himself having to convince his father that what he was doing did not mean that he was "in trouble at school."

"Okay, I'll schedule it for tomorrow."

James returned to his classroom. As Juan and I hurried back to the cafeteria, he said, "You know, some parents don't understand that this is a good thing to get a letter." And then he added ominously, "You don't know how some parents are." The way he said it made me wonder if James' father did more than "holler" at him.

The Pro-Social Action Report Forms that Jim Reynolds shared with me every day for my research project described several nonviolent conflicts I thought could have been mediated if the students had chosen to do so. Peer mediators also noticed unmediated conflicts and brought the point to our "Issues and Concerns" discussion in the after-school program. Peer mediation was a new program, we reasoned, and it was taking time for students to understand and trust both the mediators and the process. We were averaging one mediation every two and a half days, but it was difficult to figure out how that should be interpreted, or if it should be interpreted at all. Cristine Madison was typical of the trained mediators who wanted to practice their skills and strategies and were frustrated by reporting for duty and being told that there were no mediations scheduled She wrote in her journal: "On Wednesday, I was on duty with Natalia and *no one* came. We got kind of bored." A tension seemed to grow from the perception that conflicts existed, but that some students were wary of using mediation to resolve them.

About a month after the incident with James, I received a request written by Diane Fonsberg, a fifth-grade student complaining about being bothered during the school's breakfast program by a fourth-grade girl, Ada May Jones. When I found Ada May in the library, I drew her aside and told her about the mediation request because Diane had checked off "Haven't asked" under "Agreed to mediate" on the form (see Figure 7.6). Ada May's eyes widened as she said, "I know what that's about. She's always botherin' *me*, makin' faces an' all."

"Diane wants to sit down and talk it out with you in mediation."

"Naaa-uhhh," she sang, then added for emphasis, "I ain't gettin' in *no* trouble at home over *her!*"

I needed to know more about her reason. "Do you mean the letter we send home would get you into trouble?"

"Uh-huh." She nodded, then looked at the floor.

Ada May was the only one to refuse to try mediation during the screening process when I asked each student about their willingness to mediate a dispute. But my sense was that her refusal represented more than one student's feelings toward "the letter home." I needed to find out more about the punishments that seemed to overwhelm and frighten students who imagined their parents receiving our letter. I asked seven mediators individually and privately what those consequences might be. Their responses included parents' "grounding" them; preventing them "from seeing the other disputant"; transferring them "to another school"; never letting them "go back to mediation again"; and "getting angry" over their participation in a mediation—"hitting," "spanking," "beating," "yelling," "putting them in a corner for thirty minutes," "locking them in their bedroom without television." One mediator told how much she dreaded being "teased" by siblings.

I decided to take this issue to the next after-school program. We sat in a circle and, without mentioning names, I described Ada May's refusal to mediate and then asked, "What do you think she meant?"

Ricky Villatoro was the first one to start the discussion, which was unusual because he was normally quiet for most of our discussions. "She doesn't want her mother to know that she was in a talking fight with someone else."

Billy Glenn added quickly, "Maybe her mother is real strict, and she didn't want her to know about it because she might get into more trouble."

Kristi Tesadore's interpretation came next: "I think that maybe she doesn't want her mom to get in trouble with the school because maybe she worries a lot."

Sean Boudreau responded to Kristi's word "worry" and said, "Maybe she's having a hard time in her family right now. You get like you don't want to hear more bad news. You're sick of it—more bad news. You just don't want to tell parents because you don't want them to get more hurt."

Elizabeth Garrett brought up another possibility: "I *know* parents who think their kid is perfect. Then the kid gets into trouble and that kid doesn't want a letter home so that [she assumes a parent's voice], 'Well, what the heck is *my* perfect *child* doing using a program like this? She *never* gets in trouble.' On the other hand, the parent could know that the kid had a problem and it's solved."

The next comment drew an audible gasp from Sean, while everyone else stared at the speaker, Elaine Lindquist. "Well, this isn't really about the kid not wanting to mediate, but I don't think we should send a letter home." Three beats of silence filled the air and then her question: "Why do *they* need to know?"

T. J. Jackson calculated the effect of what Elaine was suggesting and spoke rapidly and loudly, as was his habit when he became excited: "When kids find out that no letter gets sent home, they'll pick mediation because they might not get into trouble for that. Say they get into a pushing fight—you said we could take pushing fights, right? You've got this choice: go to Mr. Reynolds or go to mediation. What would *you* do?" At this, he thrust his pencil into the air and pointed to all of us. "What would *you* rather do—go to Mr. Reynolds or go to mediation and get no letter?" He relaxed his hands in an "I rest my case" gesture as Cristine Madison put forth a possible solution, "Could we ask the disputants if they *want* a letter sent home, or could it depend on the conflict?"

Natalia Durgin looked at her and wagged her head. "They will *always* say no! Is the kid going to say, 'I want a letter sent home to my mother?' I think that kids don't want a letter because parents usually think that when they get a letter, it's bad. Most of the time when it goes [assuming an official voice] 'To the parent or guardian of,' it always looks bad. I've only gotten a letter home from Mr. Reynolds' office once, and it wasn't bad. And my mother said, 'All right, what did you do *this time?*' And I didn't even do anything wrong!"

Richard Walker adjusted his glasses and spoke next. "I have two things [to say] about the letter. I have been to Mr. Reynolds' office about five times." Chuckles bounced around the room. He acknowledged them with a smile and went on. "If you *just go* to his office for something you didn't even do—like my whole bus stop went there because of one person teasing another and there was fighting involved. And if you go to Mr. Reynolds' office, he sends a letter home and it becomes more like *not what you did or didn't do,* but 'your child *has been involved*' in this whole fight. And I wasn't even involved in the fight, and he sends home an entire thing with every detail of what happened. The other thing is I think I agree with Cristine that it depends, but [disputants] shouldn't decide—*we* should if it's not serious enough [to send a letter home]."

Kristi interjected, "Mr. Reynolds punishes you for being human! People have problems, you know."

After nearly falling out of his chair with agitation waiting for Richard and Kristi to finish, T. J. began, "If I'm going to get a letter sent home from a pushing fight—this is me—I'd rather duke it out and get a letter home from Mr. Reynolds."

After listening to the issues raised, Billy Glenn raised his hand. "If kids got into a conflict, they would take the easy way out, and we'd get a lot of business." Then his brow furrowed as he said, "We still should send a letter."

Ricky, who had started our discussion, added a piece of information to our data bank. "Someone told me that he won't go to mediation because the letter gets sent home."

But Kristi put herself in a parent's shoes and said, "I think it's better that we send the letter so that parents know what's going on at school." She then assumed an adult voice and intoned, "What happened at school today?" Switching on an innocent child role, she widened her eyes and said, "'Ohhhh, nothing.' Parents won't know!"

Natalia added, "I think people are petrified to have the letter sent home. If the kid is really honest, the first thing you do when you get home is tell what happened. Like when I go home, it's like, 'Guess what!'"

Richard connected to Natalia's use of "petrified" and shared this story: "I think it's like I get used to getting bad notes home for being a bad student. Most of the parents think it's trouble when they get a note, like one that had 'To the parents of Richard Walker.' And I was really scared 'cause I thought it was about a fight I just had. But it was just that I didn't have my physical." His last sentence elicited an empathic, relieved laugh from the mediators in the circle. "If we do a note home, it should be more . . ." Here Richard paused and opened a new window of thought for everyone in the room ". . . telling it's from mediation."

At this point, I wondered out loud, "Isn't the letter already from mediation? I'm confused."

T. J. and other peer mediators then instructed me about the meanings that a piece of paper held and some possibilities for transforming it. He began, "Most kids think when it's addressed to parents that the kid's in trouble, and they chuck it away or hide it. Why don't we address it to the kid?"

Elizabeth responded to T. J. and showed me that the key dilemma was still present. "To the kid *and his parents*. I have an idea. The two mediators sign the letter at the bottom. It seems like you [here she looked directly at me] are sitting there with us, and *we are running it.* Some parents might think it's that *you're* doing all this, and *we are*. It will also seem a little less *formal because it's teacher language,* like"—here she added a ponderous tone to her voice—"Dear Mr. and Mrs. So-and-So."

The discussion went on until we all agreed that "the letter home" as it existed would be eliminated. When we met the following Thursday, I divided the mediators into groups of three to brainstorm lists of "what, if anything, might replace the letter." Some of their ideas would have put to shame the college's marketing majors, who usually sat in the same chairs.

Their proposals included sending pictures of flowers and rainbows ("They mean peace and happiness"); conferring a "mediation diploma with the problem on the back"; giving away stickers; offering "treats—not doggy treats," clarified Natalia; giving a dollar, a "fake mediation dollar bill" or a "mediation scratch ticket"; having disputants write out their own problem, do the follow-up at home and return it themselves; sending a "go-home mediation kit" with instructions to get four chairs and talk out a problem—included would be a diploma that said,

"You have graduated from mediation school"; giving disputants a pen with our symbol on it; sending cards or certificates that said, "Great job! We're proud of you!"

When Jasmine Hernandez noted, "This is getting expensive," Elaine brightened and said, "We could have a fund-raiser!"

Sean was still wrestling with who would know about the conflict: "We could give a letter with the top part folded over and taped. Kids could open it and it would say congratulations and all good stuff. On the bottom, it could say: *Parents, do not open.* It gives kids confidence. And the other half could be 'To the Parents' with a description of the problem and the agreement."

T. J. thought for a moment and said, "Not everybody is as honest as Sean is. I don't like the 'To the Parents.' Some kids are going to open that part to see what it says." Here T. J. pantomimed unfolding a paper and sneaking a peek at it.

Sean persisted: "Then on the bottom, put 'Hey, you're not in trouble. Don't worry! We sent this letter to your parents because we want to notify them that *you* solved the problem.'"

Time had run out and we scurried to line up and get outside to meet rides or walk home. That week, I worked on a certificate that seemed to combine several ideas the mediators were trying to communicate (Figure 9.1). I brought a draft to them the next Thursday for their response. Kelly began by saying, "I like how it's the clipboard because it's something that we use." Sean said, "This is exactly what I meant! [He repeats this and then puts in hands and arms in baseball's "safe" position.] Everything is A-okay. If I was a kid, I would definitely want this sent home to my parents." When I told him that, because of our discussion the previous week, I thought we could let each disputant decide whether or not to take it, he said, "Oh."

D. J. and T. J. asked about having mediators sign the certificates. I told them that I had thought about that because of what Elizabeth had said the week before (". . . we are running this"), but that I had decided not to put individual names on the certificate. Sean said to them, "Yeah, you might not want your name out there where you don't know about it. If the kid gets into trouble, the parents might see your name and come asking you about it. They might get mad and try to shut [us] down." Natalia added, "Maybe [parents] have something against peer mediation or might not know much about it and wonder, 'What's this kid telling my kid what to do for?'"

On the following Monday, May 24, I visited the ten classrooms with the purpose of giving students a mediation progress report. I told each class that since the program had begun in February, there had been twenty-eight requests for mediations for reasons such as teasing, name-calling, threats, borrowing things without asking, and not keeping promises. I asked students to describe what they thought happened during a mediation and listed the steps in order on chart paper. When they said, "And then you send a letter home," I told them that there was going to be a change in the program. I finished by saying, "What is helping us make this decision is that the mediators and I think that some students are staying away from mediation because of the letter home." I noticed how students nodded in agreement when they heard the last part of my announcement. "Instead, we

Figure 9.1 Certificate of Congratulations for Problem Solvers

will offer you a certificate to take *if you want it.*" At this point, I showed students the blue certificate.

By the end of that day, there were five referrals for mediations in my mailbox. *Between then and the close of school in June, there was an average of more than one mediation a day.* This was a quantitative difference that seemed to be related to one factor—the letter home. However, twenty-five out of thirty disputants opted to take a certificate at the close of the follow-up interview. Did they take *it* home? The answer to that question could become the focus of yet another study, but it made me wonder how students and parents viewed school-to-home communication in Hampton's culture and what that meant.

In the introduction to *The Moral Life of Children,* Robert Coles (1986) discussed his interest in the ways that children are "caught between the complex and often contradictory inclinations" of adults (p. 6). "The letter home" was a communication that seemed to create a host of dilemmas from the mediators' and disputants' points of view. I had inadvertently introduced these dilemmas into the program by sending a double message to students: "Peer mediation is confidential, and you are trusted to create and keep fair agreements; however, I will send your parents a letter about mediation and your agreement, just in case you can not be trusted to do either or both."

It is important to understand that this is not a warning against sending letters to parents because of events at Hampton or a proposition that children should not face consequences for harmful behavior. Rather, I hope that it is viewed as an explanation of what it might mean to students when schools communicate with their parents.

The mediators seemed to assume that virtually any communication from school would be interpreted by parents as negative feedback about students' behavior. Misinterpretation of the mediation letter, according to Elizabeth and Richard, was fueled by its "official" look and language (To the Parents of . . .) which could lead disputants and parents to confuse it with a discipline report from Mr. Reynolds. The relieved laughter that followed Richard's story spoke volumes about the mediators' empathy for him and his anxiety over the contents of the dreaded letter, which turned out to be about his physical. It appeared that Hampton students believed letters from school meant trouble for them, and that could have had an impact on their decision to mediate a dispute.

To Send or Not to Send

Moral conflicts of no small proportion rose to the surface when Elaine stated, ". . . I don't think we should send a letter home . . . Why do *they* need to know?" The mediators' responses suggested that to continue sending a letter home from the mediation program might result in compounded and undesirable consequences for the hapless student. Should they risk the possibilities of upsetting parents (Sean's perception of "more bad news") and getting students into trouble with their parents by continuing to send a communication home?

First, as T. J. reasoned, disputing students might reason that no matter what conflict-solving route they chose, they would "get a letter sent home" so they might just as well opt for violence and "duke it out." This would certainly conflict with a belief that is central to mediation Discourse: we want people to choose talk, not violence, to resolve their disputes.

Second, if students had a problem that was not serious enough to reach the office (students called a dispute like Ada May and Diane's a "talking fight"), then it might go unmediated because of the fear of the letter home, as Ricky suggested. The dramatic increase in referrals after I visited classrooms to announce the end of "the letter home" supports that possibility. Students appeared to be sending a return message to me: "Trust us to solve our conflicts without *any* adult intervention, or we will think twice about using this process." Some students' interpretation of "without adult intervention" was clearly different from mine. Confidential meant *no* parents, unless *students* chose to inform them. Only when it seemed as if their point of view was being taken seriously did they change from resistance to acceptance.

Not sending a letter home, on the other hand, also had its disadvantages. T. J. and Billy seemed to think that it was an invitation for some students to take "the easy way out," as if some disputants were also being "morally scrutinized" for a certain lack of character (Coles 1986; see also Chapter 6). They appeared to believe that justice might not be served if *some* parents were not informed about their children's conflicts. Could it mean that they believed "kids only" input into an agreement might not equal adult punishment? It seemed that the mediators were using beliefs and expectations from a more entrenched system of justice (and one with which they seemed to have had more experience) and trying to fit them together with the Discourse of mediated cooperative problem solving. Cristine and Richard were at odds over who should have the right to decide about sending any communication home; she believed in the students' right to self-determination, while he believed that mediators should hold that power over disputants. A question I failed to ask Richard was "How will *you* decide which parents will be informed?"

A second disadvantage seemed to be linked to Kristi's, Billy's, and Sean's perception of parents' right to know what happened to their children in school. When Coles (1986) interviewed children, he found that they talked of their struggles with similar issues: "the tension between loyalty to one's friends and loyalty to one's own memories, habits, yearnings; the tension between one's competitive side and one's regard for others; the tension between one's wish to win and one's willingness to help others" (p. 142). There appeared to be a conflict between their sense of loyalty to their parents and to their peers; it was a conflict that seemed to be further complicated by their belief in self-determination and a growing awareness of differing circumstances among disputants.

To Sign or Not to Sign

Mediators wrote their names on the agreement at the beginning of the mediation, along with disputants' names, but they did not sign the letter home. To sign or not to sign documents, such as letters or certificates, appeared to be viewed differently by mediators. They moved between wanting recognition outside Hampton's walls (Elizabeth's "We are running it") and fearing it (Sean's "[Parents] might get mad and shut us down" and "If the kid gets into trouble, the parents might see your name and come asking you about it"). Elizabeth and T. J. seemed to feel that inaccurate program ownership information was being communicated because the letter was signed only by Mr. Reynolds and me, and not by them. My rationale for signatures was based again on an adult's perspective; it was an assurance to other adults that the mediation program was sanctioned by the school. Elizabeth's and T. J.'s statement was another "wake-up call" for me because of my assumption that the mediation program generally worked to enhance students' self-esteem by empowering them to solve their own disputes. The specific message I was sending by not having their signatures on letters and documents, according to Elizabeth and T. J., was one that compromised their ownership in the program.

Searching for Solutions

The mediators' solutions suggested their awareness of a communication gap between home and school. Sean, who contributed many ideas to the group during brainstorming, seemed to maintain a position to send something home based on his loyalty to parents and their right to know. He seemed to be saying: "Inform parents in a positive way about the dispute, and you will be educating families about the mediation process." Up to that point, our efforts had included the induction ceremony, which included two role plays and was shown several times on the local access cable channel; an appearance by six mediators and me on the school-oriented cable television show (see Chapter 8); three local newspaper articles; two sparsely attended parents' nights; two items in Hampton's monthly newsletters; a paragraph in the Student Handbook; and a handout (see Figure 2.1) included in every letter home.

In their efforts to grapple with the perceived communication gap that "the letter home" exposed, mediators favored making it easy and appealing for disputants to choose mediation to solve their conflicts. Their suggestions went right to the heart of the problem: *until culture-bound attitudes toward conflict are changed, mediation might be misunderstood.* Their methods to connect home, school, and neighborhood Discourses tapped into the mainstream culture's pleasure symbols: scratch tickets, money, and stickers. They could be described as attempting to make mediation "user friendly" by supplying parents with a "go-home-mediation kit."

The mediators also seemed to understand the powerful role that language played in their bid to educate students and adults about mediation. Richard's astute example from a discipline report showed his sensitivity to the subtle ways words are used to implicate students ("Your child has been involved . . ."). Sean's insistence on using phrases that "say congratulations and all good stuff" to assure the children and "give them confidence" revealed a keen understanding of mediation's rhetoric.

Those two after-school sessions were crucial to my understanding of Hampton's peer mediation program. Sending "a letter home," which included the disputants' agreement, seemed to send a mixed message to some of Hampton's students—"You are trusted, but not completely." Since mediation is voluntary, some students chose not to mediate their disputes. Hampton's peer mediators grappled with a complex set of ethical dilemmas that emerged around the issue of confidentiality and trust when they considered the impact of not sending a communication home. They appeared to move between their loyalty to parents, which included their right to know about their children's experiences, and fear of being overpowered and unjustly punished for doing a good thing—peacefully resolving a conflict using mediation.

Expecting Program Changes

Students are expert readers of home and school culture who are aware of power imbalances that exist between themselves and adults. It is necessary to engage students in discussions while observing their reactions to program features, such as Hampton's letter home. Show them that you are listening by working with them to revise their program. You are a "guide on the side" in these discussions as you weigh how changes will be consistent with mediation process and think about how revisions will be interpreted by students, parents, administrators, and teachers.

The "they" in Elaine's question, "Why do *they* need to know?" could have referred to any adults, not just parents. A decision I made about disclosure of the agreement had the effect of keeping students away from the process. In a Spring 1987 "Issue/Response" column of *NAME News*, the editors wrote,

Many school mediation programs struggle with the balance between maintaining confidentiality to protect students and the administrator's need to know . . . about disputes which have come before mediation. It is not an easy balance to keep; it does not readily translate into school policy. And it has lasting implications not only for students and administrators, but for teachers and parents as well. (p. 4)

The editors then posed a set of questions designed to raise issues of disclosure, some of which I share here:

Do schools notify parents about mediated agreements?

Do mediated agreements become part of the school record, and if so, what is the school's ownership of these agreements?

Is one of the goals of school mediation programs student empowerment, and if so, how can this be reconciled with the administrator's need to provide a safe school?

As I worked with students to maintain Hampton's peer mediation program, questions helped me to focus on the shared decision-making process that developed as we worked to make mediation a permanent and useful part of the school's culture:

When students talk about the program, are there "hot spots"—subjects that students, staff, or parents see as problematic?

Looking at various features of the program, what would be the effect of revisions?

How will students have input to changes?

A Step Back to Reflect

Interpersonal conflict is often perceived as undesirable and destructive, while cognitive conflict is recognized as necessary to one's learning process (Piaget 1975). However, interpersonal conflict is a natural and necessary part of living and learning. Widespread acceptance of the latter view will require a revision of culture-bound attitudes toward conflict itself, especially conflicts at school. Hampton's peer mediation program was three years old when the following incident occurred.

The annual PTO spaghetti supper was in progress with hundreds of parents and students feasting on pasta with meat sauce, bread, salad, and cookies. The event attracts the largest number of parents and students. Fourth-grade teacher Diane Tierney was walking toward the restroom behind a mother and her third-grade son. She saw the boy stop in front of the "March Is Mediation Month—Meet Your Mediators" bulletin board in the foyer.

Pointing to the array of photographs of students wearing blue tee shirts, he said, "Mom, these are the peer mediators."

"What do they do?"

"They help people solve conflicts."

"Well, I don't ever want to see *your* picture up there."

"No, Mom, they *help* people solve conflicts."

"And I said I don't want to see your picture up there."

In spite of the mediation program's three-year tenure, was there a revision on the part of this parent's perception of what it means to have a conflict in a school with a peer mediation program? No. The word seemed to remain a red flag for her, in spite of her son's effort to explain the concept of mediation. Was this discouraging to Diane and me? Yes. But it highlighted the fact that change takes time, and we cannot assume that efforts to educate others will reach everyone.

C H A P T E R   T E N

≈ ≈

Program Changes: Finding and Solving Problems

Could We Talk About . . .

Time and *space* carry special meanings in peer mediation Discourse. A program coordinator's initial challenge is to locate mediations somewhere within the confines of a school's tightly woven web of schedules and spaces. *When* will mediations take place—lunch, recess, study hall, activity period, after school? And *where*—cafeteria, playground, library corner, empty classroom, storage closet?

During the 1991–92 school year, when Jim Reynolds and I first discussed my plan to schedule mediations during lunch and recess, the periods were thirty minutes each. This hour was the students' only school-sanctioned, unstructured socialization time, but I reasoned that if mediation offered students an opportunity to deal with interpersonal conflicts, then they would need to invest their lunch or recess time in solving their problem. I would also be fulfilling my promise to parents, teachers, and administrators that the mediation program would not interfere with academic instruction (see Chapter 2). Choosing lunch and recess seemed to hold another advantage. Students seeing disputants carrying their lunch trays to unoccupied tables on the far side of the cafeteria might send an explicit message of support for the new program: "We have chosen mediation to try to resolve a dispute." As with the letter home (see Chapter 9), I was not seeing the situation from a Hampton student's point of view.

Jim Reynolds was operating from yet another perspective in June when he made a change in the schedule that would go into effect during the upcoming 1992–93 school year. His role as Hampton's assistant principal meant he was the final stop on matters of scheduling and discipline. He said, "Seventy-five percent of the problems happened [ended up in the office as discipline referrals] during the last ten minutes of lunch and recess." Reynolds perceived the final segment of lunch as "setting [students] up, because they sit there with nothing to do." Consequently he "eliminated those two times by reducing both periods to twenty minutes." He seemed to believe that shortening the time would result in controlling students' behavior, or least keeping them out of trouble serious enough to warrant sending them to the office.

My experiences as a mediator made me wonder if the abbreviated lunch and recess periods would have an effect on the program as I had envisioned it. I thought that it might take more time for students to talk out complex problems rooted in a long history of misunderstandings and mistrust. But I could not argue the point with Jim Reynolds since the program did not yet exist. When Hampton's peer mediators began their duties in February 1993, I scheduled one pair for twenty minutes in the cafeteria and a second team on the playground.

It did not take long before the topic of time was brought up in our weekly after-school program. A discussion began when the mediators and I noticed that nine mediations had taken two lunch periods to resolve, while two others had taken three periods.

Kristi asked, "Could we talk about expanding time, then? I started a mediation, but it took two or three lunch periods before it was resolved."

Natalia supported her. "We're not getting to help solve that problem if they're leaving before we're done."

Kristi and Natalia appeared to see themselves as individually responsible for following a mediation to the end and to believe that the truncated lunch periods impaired their ability to help disputants. Because the program's rotating schedule could not accommodate mediators staying with disputants whenever there were longer mediations, it became necessary for mediators and disputants to step in and out of the process.

Crystal added, "Sometimes, when it takes more than one time to do a mediation, some of the problems are real interesting and I want to know more about how they solved it." If the roles of mediator and disputant can be described as "one-caring" and "cared-for," then she expected "reciprocity . . . what it is that the cared-for contributes to the relation" (Noddings 1984, p. 4). Crystal seemed frustrated by the time constraints because she expected to learn something about problem solving from the disputants.

Billy said, "When we picked up with them the next day, we started the introduction and they said, 'We did that already.' And we said, 'Sorry, we have to do this part.'"

Several issues seemed to be emerging, so I said, "There is a lot going on here, isn't there? What are some ways we could solve these problems?"

Billy thought a minute and said, "Maybe the next mediators could just pick up from where the others left off. They could mark on the agreement form how far they got" (see Figure 7.4).

Natalia blurted out, "But then, we have no defense if they start to interrupt. How can *I say*, 'You agreed not to interrupt'?"

Elizabeth pointed out, "Well, you can say, 'You agreed to the rules yesterday.'" Natalia didn't look satisfied.

I looked around. "How does that sound?" There were murmurs of agreement. Then I suggested, "If you are unsure about disputants remembering the rules, could you ask them to tell *you* the rules they agreed to and remind them of the ones they don't remember?"

We finally constructed a solution that had pairs of mediators deciding whether or not to restate the rules of the introduction or have disputants restate the ones that they remembered, as well as leaving the agreement marked in the margins "We left off here" or "Start here" or "Start brainstorming solutions" (see Figure 7.2). I offered to ask teachers on lunch duty if they could let disputants get their lunch ahead of the other students in order to make the most of the twenty minutes.

Elaine turned us in another direction. "I was wondering if we could *not* have mediation during everyone's meal. Some say, 'I want to eat.'" She seemed to be aware that the eating ritual might be viewed by some students as an inappropri-ate time for problem solving. I saw her point immediately and thought about conflict discussions becoming emotional. "When should we offer mediations?"

"Recess!" came the chorus.

Elaine and Richard echoed each other's reply: "They don't want to give up their recess!"

It seemed to be true. Many mediators had had recess duty and noticed that mediations did not take place during play time.

I had also noticed students' resistance to giving up their recess. When I approached disputants on the playground to stop and do the follow-up interview (see Figure 7.5), or to mediate a dispute and give up their play time to go off into a quiet section of the playground, they frequently said, "Can't we do it at lunch tomorrow?" When time had run out and I had given disputants the option to continue it at recess, everyone chose the next lunch. With barely fifteen minutes to play, they were even reluctant to do follow-up interviews during their recess. In a school day that was structured to account for every minute of state-mandated instructional time, even ten or fifteen minutes of unstructured play was valued by students who must *voluntarily* bring their disputes to media-tion. Teachers, administrators, and peer mediators asked the question, "Why don't more students use mediation?" It helped me understand how some stu-dents, who resisted using the process to solve problems, could be seeing their choice as being between work and play. Again, my assumption that they would readily give up play time was based on an adult's point of view.

I showed my frustration. "So, what you're saying is that students don't want to give up lunch or recess. But they have to give up something if they want to solve their problem. An angel won't come down from heaven and do it for them. It will take time."

"Well, then," reasoned Kristi, "we should have it all day long." Laughter erupted. She held up her hand in a "just listen to this" gesture. "Kids could do work in their classrooms, but when a conflict comes up they could mediate it right then and there. Any time. That would solve the problem totally."

"Kristi, that's makes sense," I said, "but it would mean that every classroom would need at least two mediators. Right now, one room only has one mediator, and the third grades who eat at second lunch don't have any."

She thought a moment and said, "There could be two sets of mediators on duty and one could do the first half of the day and the second set could do the second half." I was impressed that a ten-year-old problem solver could concep-tualize revising the new program in this manner. Her "right then and there" related to Johnson and Johnson's (1991) recommendation that each teacher "train all students to be mediators," and then refer all conflicts to them (p. 1:15; see Chapter 5).

Natalia filled in Kristi's idea with a logistical detail. "The teacher could call the office and say, 'I need two mediators to come.' Some problems don't take long, so we could do it and go back to class."

Billy took in the proposal, thought ahead, and posed this scenario, "But when two mediators are on call, it could keep them running all the time."

The agitation in Sean's voice reflected the multiple perspectives he was taking. "In and out of their rooms, going back and forth. Like, *what is going on here?!* We would go crazy, pulling our hair out. It's a good idea, but mediators have work to do. Say there's a really important math test, and I happen to be on duty and get called to do a mediation. Then I go to get the other kid and have to interrupt the teacher."

T. J. predicted, "Some teachers could say, 'No, you can't go because you have work to do.'"

Sean saw that his being on call would interfere with his own responsibilities as a student and that he would also have to interrupt a teacher to carry out his duties and possibly be considered a troublemaker himself. He seemed to realize that although he played an additional, empowering role in school (Davis and Porter 1985a), it did not come within the mediators' power to challenge teachers and administrators who had control over classrooms and schedules.

Natalia spoke again. "I'm starting to agree with T. J. and Sean more now because if you happen to be a mediator, kids in class might get jealous and say, 'You can get out of class any time, and we have to stay.' I wouldn't want that to happen." Natalia seemed sensitive to a "change of status" as Erickson (1984) defined it, albeit it for high school students:

> This holds true in such high school rituals as awarding athletic letters and initiation into a national honor society, which publicly acknowledge that not only have certain individuals entered new and higher statuses but that they also have entered new forms of social relations with former peers, who are now outsiders of lower relative status. (p. 57)

It seemed that solutions to the problem had to be in line with students' perception of themselves as "normal" kids, meaning that they did not want to disrupt their student role to assume their mediator role and pay the price of unwanted status among friends. The discussion made me look harder at my adult agenda for improving students' self-esteem and leadership opportunities and made me understand how they wanted to be perceived by their peers.

The clock forced an end to our discussion. "Five minutes more. Does anyone want to add anything else to the issue of time?" I asked.

D. K. responded, "Some disputants are very impatient during mediations. They look around. They don't understand that when we ask them questions, it takes time to write down what they say" (see Figure 7.4). When disputants were "looking around" or at their friends, mediators interpreted it negatively. D. K. appeared to expect disputants to reciprocate by mirroring her own professional body language during each step of the ritual.

Richard said, "The thing I didn't like was when they kept telling us to skip everything. They said, 'We already know that part. Skip down.'" While I interpreted that as a good sign (as students became more familiar with mediation language and process, they wanted to get on with the business of problem solving), Richard did not. He interpreted it as disputants' breaking a rule of interaction behavior, as described by sociologist Erving Goffman (1967):

> These rules, when followed, determine the evaluation he will make of himself and his fellow-participants in the encounter, the distribution of his feelings, and the kinds of practices he will employ to maintain a specified and obligatory kind of ritual equilibrium. (p. 45)

When faced with impatient disputants, Richard perceived it as an erosion of his effectiveness or a challenge to his competence and ability to control the interaction. I recalled my experience during adult mediations, which frequently take three or more hours, when I felt similar pressure brought on by the small gesture of disputants' glancing at their watches.

When viewing their part in a two- or three-day mediation, Billy and Natalia appeared to equate the repetition of the introduction with either individual trust building or control insurance ("We have no defense if they start to interrupt"). Elizabeth, on the other hand, perceived disputants' agreeing to the rules the day before as adequate to get on with the business at hand: having *disputants work on solving their problem.* To Elizabeth's way of thinking, if a mediation were likened to a bus trip, a change of drivers would not necessarily compromise the success of the trip. In other words, the group or "team" identity (Goffman 1959, pp. 78– 92) of peer mediators became more important than their individual one. If students viewed all mediators as trained, competent, neutral third parties, then the process, not the individual mediators, became the glue of the experience.

What began as Kristi's request to "talk about expanding time" brought the issue to a head. A show of support came immediately from the lunch-duty teachers, who saw no problem with allowing disputants to get their lunches as soon as they entered the cafeteria. The next week, I drafted a letter that explicitly stated one outcome of the peer mediators' decision making and sent it to the faculty and administration:

> Beginning at today's first and second lunches, there will be two pairs of peer mediators on duty in the cafeteria and none at either recess. In the weeks since we have had recess duty, there has been little mediation work to do. On the other hand, we are frequently backlogged with mediations and follow-up interviews during lunch times. Students seem to be willing to mediate a dispute during lunch time, but they are less willing to give up their twenty minutes of playtime. As the good weather approaches, it becomes more understandable, so we are making this adjustment. The peer mediators' decision began with a suggestion by Kristi Tesadore. We think it makes sense to give it a try.
>
> If there are any questions or concerns about this or any aspect of the program, please don't hesitate to see me. The referral system seems to be working out really well in terms of providing a way for classroom disputes to come to mediation. Our thanks to all of you who are making it possible for students to have access to this process.

The letter was intended to work on two levels: first, it communicated a program change to teachers and administration, and second, it gave credit to the peer mediators for developing a change in the program. Eliminating recess as a time for mediations was one of several changes originating from discussions that took place during the weekly after-school program.

Responding to a Variety of Program Needs

What becomes a solution one year may need to be changed in the next. What works in one school may not in another. Researcher David Fetterman (1989) wrote about drop-out prevention programs, but his observation can be applied to peer mediation programs: "Programs, like people, adapt to their environment. Expecting a program to replicate itself like a cell is unrealistic and dooms the process before it begins" (p. 127). Not all changes were driven by student response to the program. Here are brief descriptions of revisions in Hampton's program that have occurred over three years. It may help to learn about our changes if you become invested in starting up a program. You will need to anticipate and encourage change as you work to build and maintain a program. If you have mediation program experience, you may recognize some familiar issues.

Funding support. When I implemented Hampton's program, I began it as a research project for my dissertation. There was no budget. I had paid for my own basic mediation training, but was granted support by Riverton State to attend two NAME conferences. Hampton's Parent-Teacher Organization paid for the plain blue tee shirts that each mediator wore when they went on duty. I paid for weekly after-school program snacks of soda and cookies.

If a program is to survive its first year and continue to function, the network of adults invested in it must grow (Cohen 1987a). The identity of your key coordinator carries with it the life of your program. However, Ann Ellsworth (1993) concluded in her cultural study of an urban middle school program that "a program cannot be institutionalized if it rests solely on the extraordinary gifts and energy of one person, no matter how desirable it is to have such a person heading the implementation" (p. 208). For me that network of support came from John Grayson, Diane Tierney, and Larry Jamison, three Hampton teachers who became interested in peer mediation as they watched the program take hold.

Riverton's school department and Riverton State College agreed to fund basic training for three Hampton teachers and for several others in the city who were interested in starting up programs in their schools. Every year since, Riverton School Department has included funds in its budget for mediation programs, which help pay for materials, provide stipends for three classroom teachers who are coaches, and provide snacks. The coordinator's position has become part of my teaching load in the education department. The three coaches and I are a team; we plan and teach the peer mediators and share program responsibilities. We believe that we provide a model for students who may only have seen their teachers and administrators working either in isolation or within the confines of their hierarchical relationships.

Adult volunteer support and safety issues. By definition, peer mediation means students work toward resolving conflicts *without adult intervention*. However, adults play a critical role in a peer mediation program. To define it becomes yet another task that holds implications for the future of a program.

Jamie Gilson's (1991) *Sticks and Stones and Skeleton Bones* offers a view of adult supervision that left me feeling skeptical. In it, Miss Ivanovitch, the teacher/trainer, sits nearby grading papers while the mediation is in progress. Hobie, a fifth-grade disputant, "couldn't tell if she was listening or not" (p. 106). Her reason for being there was that it was the inexperienced peer mediators' first mediation, and that she was there to give them moral support as they waded through the conflict. When Miss Ivanovitch leaves to pick up the class from gym, she tells the mediators and disputants to finish the mediation and come to class (p. 119). When the principal comes upon the students and says, "You're unsupervised," the peer mediator answers, "We're trusted, sir" (p. 124).

While confidentiality is a crucial part of mediations, students' personal safety must be ensured. Adult supervision should not be equated with students' not being trusted. In Chapter 4, I pointed to the ethical issue surrounding the level of adult preparation in order to understand and support students as they experience the joys and discomforts of becoming a neutral third party in dispute resolution. My experience has led me to tie this decision to the issue of personal safety. Hampton's peer mediators *do not* go on duty unless there is an adult volunteer *within sight, not sound,* of the mediation table.

Even after four years, one of the questions most frequently asked by mediators, students, and parents has been: "What happens if a fight breaks out during mediation? Will I [or my child] be safe?" Our answer has been: "When there is any sign that physical violence is about to begin, stop the mediation immediately and get the adult." It is best not to assume that all students are experts at reading body language leading to violent behavior, so devote time to activities and discussion aimed at developing those skills.

When another related program change occurred in April 1995, the personal safety issue arose again. Hampton's peer mediators decided that being out in the open at tables might be embarrassing to some disputants. They spent two after-school program sessions designing a more private space, using temporary walls to block off the table and decorating them with the finalists' drawings from our second symbol contest. Throughout these privacy discussions, I noticed that perceived threats to personal safety continued to be raised by students: "What if a fight breaks out behind the walls?" The peer mediators were satisfied that the adult volunteer would sit alongside the area, within sight, but not sound, of the mediators and disputants.

During the first year of Hampton's program, I was the adult/coordinator/coach/researcher on duty every day with each team of peer mediators. Immersion in each role was crucial to developing my understanding of how the program was taking hold in Hampton's culture. In order to begin an analysis and interpretation of what had accumulated into mountains of data, however, it became necessary for me to reduce the number of days I spent at Hampton. At a faculty meeting, I told staff that the mediators and I needed adults to help me supervise mediations during lunch times. It would mean extra duty, and since most staff already had duty assignments, I held little hope for filling the slots that I was unable to cover. The teachers on the second lunch team offered to schedule a third teacher and rotate the duty over several days. The art teacher volunteered, and so did a special needs teacher and the librarian. When the principal from another elementary school in Riverton visited the school and was told about the Hampton teachers volunteering, he said bluntly, "My staff would never do that."

I also went to the Parent-Teacher Organization president and told her of our needs. When she brought our problem to the next meeting, five parents volunteered to work with the mediation program. I added a plea for adult volunteers at the end of the mediation permission letter (Appendix A.7). Every year presents the challenge of attracting enough dependable adults to share in the coaches' supervision of the peer mediation program. However, parent volunteers who join teachers and coaches in sacrificing their time to supervise the peer mediators send a powerful message to students: We support the mediation program and we trust you to solve your own problems.

Increasing the number of mediators. Consider changing from a limiting selection process toward preparing the maximum number of students to become peer mediators. Each year the number of students who nominated themselves as peer mediators grew, and the selection process continued to be problematic (see Chapters 5 and 6). During the first week of the 1995–96 school year, Hampton's peer mediation coaches—Diane Tierney, John Grayson, and Larry Jamison—and I met to plan a major change in the program. We decided to let all the fourth- and fifth-grade students who volunteered become peer mediators. It had taken us two years to gain the experience and confidence to prepare all students who volunteered to become mediators. After the classroom presentations in September, seven experienced peer mediators from last year's fourth-grade group interviewed the seventy-eight students who volunteered.

It is important to note that all students who initially volunteer may not become mediators. Since parental permission letters had to be returned prior to training, the number fell to sixty-four. Before the induction ceremony, four more students either changed their minds or brought a note from home saying that attendance in the after-school program was not possible. While it was disappointing to have students withdraw from the program for any reason, the coaches and I believed that two days of immersion in self-esteem, active listening, and mediation role-play activities was a beneficial learning experience (Davis and Porter 1985b).

Were there problems with taking large numbers of students into the program? Certainly. Four coaches became two teams who worked with two separate groups of mediators in two rooms. Peer mediators have duty only once or twice a month as compared with once or twice a week when the group was smaller. However, it is a decision that no one regrets having made.

Program changes. Try to view program changes with a positive attitude. While I struggled with my own less-than-positive attitude toward change, the peer mediators "made lemonade out of lemons" in their ability to use language to find and grapple with problems in the program. A difficult lesson for me has been learning to view problems the way the mediators perceived them—as opportunities for creative thinking. The peer mediators practiced a high level of literacy, as described by Rexford G. Brown (1991), that involved

> a process of *making meaning* and *negotiating it with others*. It is not just a set of skills useful for understanding the works and ideas of previous generations; it is a way of creating, here and now, the meanings by which individuals and groups shape their lives and plan their futures. (p. 35)

The following questions helped guide me in reflecting on my experience and may be helpful to you:

> When will peer mediators have an opportunity to discuss program issues, such as time and space?

What in-school policies are being instituted that could have an impact on the peer mediation program?

How do you view your position as being able to negotiate program needs?

Who will fulfill the functions of the coordinator's role?

What support system (funding and personnel) is necessary to help maintain the peer mediation program?

What investment in the future is your town, city, or state willing to make by funding a peer mediation program?

A Step Back to Reflect

The brittle seventy-foot white pine on the far side of our driveway seemed to be losing more limbs than usual, and its proximity to our house made John and me nervous enough to find out about cutting it down. After the arborist gave us an estimate, we asked him why the tree seemed to be dying. His answer helped me reflect on the effect of the changes that occurred over time in Hampton's peer mediation program.

"Well, your driveway looks new," he said as he surveyed the area around the tree.

I wondered what the driveway had to do with the tree. When we moved in two decades earlier, it consisted of two tire ruts. We promptly spread crushed stone in an effort to improve the look of the property. One summer we added a garage at the end of the driveway. Six months later we noticed that our snow blower would throw a plume of snow peppered with pea stone, and I came to expect the sound of pinging against the house after each New England storm. Three years ago we invested in a blacktop driveway, eliminated the pinging and inadvertently solved a drainage problem in our cellar. However, we had caused another.

"This driveway has cut off a big part of the tree's water supply. When it rains, the water can't soak into its roots," the arborist explained.

You may wonder how our driveway and tree problem relates to my analysis and interpretation of time issues in Hampton's peer mediation program. Every year, Jim Reynolds made decisions to restructure lunch and recess either by changing the length of time, the population, or the sequence of grades having lunch. On the surface, these are straightforward solutions to time and space problems administrators face every day. However, each change affected our program in significant ways that reminded me of the predictable and unpredictable consequences stemming from our decision to blacktop the driveway.

The 1994–95 school lunch and recess periods were back to thirty minutes each. Several primary teachers had requested an earlier lunch, so Jim Reynolds moved the fourth grade to the last lunch. When I scheduled peer mediators for duty, I was unable to distribute them between the two lunches. That year, we had thirty-six mediation referrals, but three-quarters of them were from the fourth lunch. That meant that some mediators were seeing the end of the year approach without ever having had a "real" mediation. Yet, they continued to give up their recess to go on duty and attended the after-school program, participating with enthusiasm (and growing skill) in each role play.

Peer Mediation Program Issues and Concerns

Name _____ Date _____

I am concerned about... My question is...

_____

_____

_____

_____

Please give this to the adult volunteer on mediation duty with you who will put it
in Dr. Ferrara's mediation envelope in the teachers' mailroom. Or you can bring it
to the after-school program this week. Your issues and concerns will be discussed
during the first part of our meeting.

Figure 10.1   Peer Mediation Program Issues and Concerns

In April 1995, an after-school program Issues and Concerns (Figure 10.1)
segment began with these questions: "What if someone wants to come to mediation, but the other disputant won't say yes? How can we help the person who
wants to talk about the problem?" "What if someone has a problem and wants
to talk about it, but can't come to mediation because it doesn't involve someone
at Hampton?" "What if people just want to get something off their chests and
don't have anyone to listen to them?"

The peer mediators, lacking the beneficial rainfall of frequent mediations
to nourish their roots, sent out a far-reaching tendril by creating an additional
role for themselves.

CHAPTER ELEVEN

≈ ≈

Peer Helpers: Finding Another Way to Care

It Started Out Like a Little Idea

It was April 1995, the third year of Hampton's peer mediation program. Four coaches and thirty mediators sat in a circle drinking soda and eating cookies at the beginning of our weekly after-school program. We were discussing the issue of low numbers of mediations during the first lunch.

This group of fourth- and fifth-grade students contained a core of experienced fifth-grade mediators, which included Pam Bonneau, Lauren Bracco, Ralph Glover, and Deven Mancini. They had moved up from fourth grade and volunteered for another year of service. Pam asked, "Why aren't people coming to mediation in first lunch?"

Larry, who was lead coach for that week, suggested, "Why don't you call on some people who may have ideas, Pam?"

Deven Mancini thought for a moment and raised her hand. Pam nodded toward her and said, "Deven."

"One of the reasons I know is this: because mediation is voluntary, one disputant wants to come but the other one doesn't. So there's no mediation."

Allison Dominico began as soon as Pam saw her hand. "That person is probably still upset about the problem and might want to talk with someone else about it."

Renee Mallory said, "Some people who might want to come to mediation could be scared that the other person will get even more mad. They could at least talk with *someone* about the problem."

Deven's face lit up as she said, "Why not have peer counselors?" Her words rose in the air and landed in a ring of excited "Yeah's!" The peer mediators' reaction seemed to show that they shared some common understanding of the term. Their talk began with a fervor of discovery that could be translated into "We're on to something."

Megan Gereaux seemed to be sensitive to how Hampton's guidance counselor might view the idea. "I don't think we should call ourselves 'counselors' because it sounds as if we're trying to take Miss Riley's job away from her."

Larry asked, "What would you suggest, Megan?"

While she took a moment to think, Lauren called out, "How about 'peer helper'?" John, Larry, Diane, and I looked at one another, knowing that the peer mediators had opened the door and were leading us and the program into another room in a house built on the same foundation of caring.

Diane said, "Each of you seems to have some idea about what you mean by peer counselor or helper. You need to talk some more and then share those ideas with the whole group. Are there some questions that will help us find out what we're thinking?"

As she stepped over to the chalkboard, Bob Lincoln raised his hand and said, *"What would mediators do as peer helpers?"*

Diane wrote while Larry, John, and I passed blank paper around the circle. "Lauren?"

"What wouldn't or couldn't mediators do as peer helpers?"

"Mr. Grayson?"

"A third thing we should find out are *questions or concerns* anyone has."

When Diane finished writing, she said, "Starting with Mr. Grayson, swing your chair around and face the person sitting on your left. You and your partner have fifteen minutes to brainstorm lists of ideas that will help to think about answers to these three questions."

When the peer mediators and coaches shared our lists during the second half of the session, we were teaching each other our perceptions of "peer helper": *What would mediators do as peer helpers?*

> Say, "We're here to help you."
> Make sure the person is there voluntarily.
> Keep neutral, don't judge.
> Keep confidentiality, except for information about drugs, alcohol, or weapons on school property, abuse, or suicide.
> Work one-on-one (one helper, one person with a problem).
> Listen to the person with the problem.
> Listen to any kind of problems, even personal, or home problems, as well as school disputes.
> Use active listening (restating).
> Ask about deep feelings.
> Be/act serious.
> Try to step into the person's shoes.
> Respect diversity (differences in ways of being and thinking).
> Help because he/she would not be holding it inside.
> Follow a guide, like the green booklet, only shorter.
> Help guide the person in ways to figure out what to do by asking, "What could you do? What else? What else?" (brainstorming).
> Have a regular duty.
> Ask open-ended questions ("Could you tell a little more about . . .?").
> Ask, "Why do you think the other person does that?"
> Ask, "What would you tell a friend who was having this problem to do?"

The list of what peer helpers would not or could not do consisted of only two items, which further indicated that they were leaning heavily on their understanding of the mediation process: They would not write an agreement; and they would not/could not give advice.

Their questions taught us about their concerns:

> How would people get to see us?
> How would people find out about our new role?

Peer Helper Request

Your name _____ Date _____

Why do you think you want to talk with a peer helper?

_____

_____

_____

_____

_____

Your teacher's name _____ *Peer helper_____
*Peer helper's name will be filled in when you get to the lunchroom.

Figure 11.1   Peer Helper Request

What if a mediator doesn't want to be a peer helper?
What kind of training would there be?
Why don't/can't we give advice?

As coaches, Larry, Diane, John, and I had the responsibility of assisting mediators in their construction of a new role. We needed to consider implications tied to their proposal and anticipate issues and concerns that might arise. Fortunately, our monthly planning meeting was scheduled for that Friday after school.

We spent the meeting assessing our needs and discovered that there were many. First, the mediators were moving full speed ahead, and we needed to slow them down. We thought that we would need to spend at least four after-school sessions exploring what it might mean to become a peer helper.

From their list of questions, we predicted that every mediator might not wish to take on this new role, so we needed a way to allow mediators to volunteer for this additional commitment *after* they understood what it entailed.

We needed a process and a set of guidelines to follow. What would it take to prepare students to become peer helpers? We would need to design role plays that could prepare them for the kinds of problems they might encounter. We wondered what kinds of problems students from Hampton's neighborhood (see Chapter 3) would talk about. One solution included inviting Clare Riley, the guidance counselor, to the next after-school program. We needed her expertise and cooperation. She was Hampton's solitary adult counselor and served over six hundred students. A peer helper program could offer an extra option to support students who needed someone to listen to them.

Finally, we would need to plan classroom presentations to help students understand what a peer helper could and could not do.

While the coaches planned, the mediators moved ahead. Within a week, Erica Kenevian, a fifth-grade mediator in Larry's class, knocked on my office door and handed me a "peer helper request form" that she had drafted on her classroom computer during writing workshop (Figure 11.1). I noticed that she had modeled it after Hampton's peer mediation request form (see Figure 7.6). When I asked her how she had come up with the idea, she responded, "We're going to need it if someone needs a peer helper." Before she turned to leave, she asked, "Should I start working on a follow-up, too?" (Figure 11.2). The new program seemed to be already established in her mind.

During that same week, Ralph Glover and Deven Mancini, fifth-grade students in John's classroom, collaborated during writing workshop on a four-step sequence that could guide the peer helper and help seeker from introduction to wrap-up (Figure 11.3). When they brought it to me in the lunchroom, I noticed that they, too, had appropriated key aspects of the peer mediation process (see Figure 7.2). I told them that I would make copies for discussion in our next after-school program. Deven suggested that, since there was no written agreement, the peer helper could offer the student a notepad to jot down possible solutions for the problem.

When fifth-grade mediator Ralph Glover later described the creation of peer helpers, he echoed each coach's thinking: "I was pretty surprised that peer mediators, not adults, made this up. It took team work and a little while to work it out. It happened that way because *we were having a problem, and then all of a sudden, it turned into peer helper.*" He added hopefully, "It's a solution that could keep growing and growing."

Lauren Bracco, another experienced fifth-grade mediator, noticed that Deven's suggestion "started out like a little idea" and grew into a new offshoot of Hampton's peer mediation program. Experienced peer mediators wanted to enlarge their capacity to practice caring, while newer members of the program wanted experience in caring. They demonstrated an ethic driven by a desire to help individuals with their problems. Peer mediation and peer helping *seemed* to fit together as the mediators used what they had learned to build a new role.

What Is Caring?

The May 1995 issue of *Phi Delta Kappan* was devoted to "Youth and Caring." In the prologue, "Why We Should Care About Caring," Joan Lipsitz wrote that the contributing authors believed "we can make schools places where people not only learn, but also construct moral lives" (p. 665). Kris Bosworth (1995), director of the Center for Adolescent Studies at Indiana University, Bloomington, interviewed middle school students in an effort to elicit their perceptions of "caring." She found that five themes emerged: helping, feelings (empathy), relationships (caring about yourself and others), values (kindness, respect, and faithfulness), and activities (spending time with someone, sharing, and listening). While four of these five themes supported ways in which Hampton's fourth- and fifth-grade peer mediators were perceiving themselves as they designed their new role, the finer points in the first theme—helping—presented a conflict between care giving and mediation Discourse.

Bosworth's middle school students perceived that helping was part of what one does when one cares. It involved forms of action ("explain work to them [classmates and friends]," "ask what the problem is, and try to help them solve it") and "provide guidance . . . by 'giving advice.'" The latter response conflicted with the belief in self-determination (the right and ability of people to solve their own problems)—one of the five principles of mediation (see Chapter

---

Peer Helper Follow-Up

1. How are things going for you, _____?
2. What ideas have you used to try to solve your problem?
3. How are your solutions working to solve the problem?
4. Do you feel that the problem is solved?
5. If not, what else could you try to solve the problem?

Figure 11.2   Peer Helper Follow-Up

4 for further discussion). It was a knot that Hampton's peer mediators kept trying to untie as they conceptualized what the role of peer helper might mean. Their choice of the word "helper" implied an active mode, yet the coaches' adherence to the mediation principle of self-determination seemed to be holding them back from that form of action.

During an after-school session devoted to peer helper issues, Pam Bonneau asked, "What if you hear the problem, and you can't tell the person what to do, but you know who could, like a teacher. Could you tell him or her what to do? Something like, 'If you wanted to, you could talk to Miss Riley.'"

John listened, then said, "Pam, that's suggesting a solution. You need to think of ways to have them come up with the idea. Without saying who the people are, you could ask, 'Are there any other people you know you can talk to besides me?' Have *them* think of others they would trust who could help them if they need more help."

Pam recognized her coach's mediation Discourse. "So, we still can't say to the person, 'Well, you can do this and that.' We're not supposed to solve the problem. They are. They're supposed to come up with ways. What if we were to say, 'Get a bigger boy to beat him up'? And then someone gets hurt and then the person comes back and says, 'Well, the peer helper told me to do it.' *Told.* And they might even think, 'I have to listen to the peer helper' and do what you say. If a peer helper offers a suggestion, the problem could get worse."

The tension between self-determination and the mediators' desire to give advice persisted once the peer helper program began. During an after-school session in early June, Deven started the Issues and Concerns segment by saying, "There's something bad about being a peer helper. I was a peer helper one day and there was this kid who was having a hard time with another kid. What was happening was that one of them wasn't doing anything, but the other one just kept bothering him. He was jumping on his back. He told me the problem, and I asked a few open-ended questions. And I listened to the problem. And then I thanked him for coming to peer helper. And I felt like I didn't *do anything*. He still had the problem. *Now* he just told someone about it."

I asked, "Did the person think of some things he might do to solve the problem?"

Deven said, "Well, umm, he did say that he didn't try mediation yet, so he was going to ask the person. And he might try to tell the teacher."

I said, "So, you *did* do something. You listened to the problem and he

Peer Helper Process

A. Introduction

Names!
Introduce yourselves to each other.
Confidentiality!
Explain that everything said is confidential (not repeated, kept secret) *except* for information about drugs, alcohol, or weapons on school property, abuse, or suicide.
Rules!
Explain that there are two rules to agree to:
- try to be honest about the problem.
- understand that peer helpers cannot give advice or tell how to solve the problem because they are neutral.
Stop!
Explain that the talk can stop at any time.

B. What Happened? (listening, restating, asking questions)

What Happened?
Ask the person what happened. Restate facts and feelings.
"So, let me see if I understand…"
"Is that right?"
"So, did you feel…?"
Helper Summaries
Summarize the entire problem, including key facts and feelings that have been described by the person.
Needs
Ask: "What do you need to happen to solve this problem?"

C. Brainstorming Solutions

The person can use a notepad to keep track of ideas.
Ask, "What *could you* do to solve this problem?" "What else?"
Remember: The goal is for the person to come up with as many ways as possible. If she/he gets stuck, ask, "What would you tell someone else who had this same problem?"
Ask: What could you do differently in the future if the same problem happens?"

D. Wrap-Up

Thank the person for coming to talk about the problem.
Tell him/her that you hope it helped and that she/he can come back any time to talk more.
Say, "In about a week, we will be scheduling a follow-up to see how it's going. Thanks again."

Figure 11.3   Peer Helper Process

thought of some possible ways to solve it. Deven, don't underestimate the power of talking and having someone to listen."

Deven's frustration came through in her voice: "I just don't feel like I've done anything. He could have come up with those ways all on his own."

I asked, "Then, what good is it to do peer helping?"

She thought for a moment and said, "Well, I thought when we were talking about [being a] peer helper, we were going to deal with more serious problems. They're getting them off their chest, but there's nothing we can do about them."

I said, "Deven, some of us are lucky. We can go to a friend and say, 'This is happening and I just need to talk about it.' But some kids don't have anybody."

Clara Binette offered her own experience and helped us understand the possible good that peer helpers might do. "Last year, I did have problems getting along. And I would have loved to have peer helpers. I was okay with going to Miss Riley 'cause she's real nice. But it would be more helpful to talk to a peer. Most kids know how I feel and even though Miss Riley did know, she really doesn't know what the world is for a child anymore. From Miss Riley's generation to our generation, there have been whole new changes. Kids do crazy things. And peer helpers, if they had been around when I had a lot of problems, I probably would have been real happy if I could have talked to one. Knowing that person is from my same generation, that person probably has gone through what I've gone through.

"My cousin died when she was two, and it bugged me for a long time. And most kids have known someone who has died. It would have been easier to have talked with someone from my own generation."

Clara helped us to appreciate how much she needed someone her own age who would listen to how she was feeling about personal issues. She provided us with an example of one who would feel relief in simply talking about a problem and not keeping intense feelings bottled up inside.

In later discussions, some peer mediators continued to feel frustrated by the tension between a mediator's need to be an impartial, empathic guide and listener, but not a giver of advice. However, they were also posing a significant question about the meaning of friendship. Should a friend give advice or push us to figure out ways to solve our problems ourselves?

Larry, Diane, John, and I considered the kinds of problems that could be brought to a peer helper. Nel Noddings (1995) wrote,

> Caring teachers must help students make wise decisions about what information they will share about themselves. On the one hand, teachers want their students to express themselves, and they want their students to trust in and consult them. On the other hand, teachers have an obligation to protect immature students from making disclosures that they might later regret. There is a deep ethical problem here . . . In reality, there is a real danger of intrusiveness and lack of respect in methods that fail to recognize the vulnerability of students . . . Teachers . . . should anticipate the tough problems that may arise. I am arguing here that it is morally irresponsible to simply ignore existential questions and themes of care; we must attend to them. But it is equally irresponsible to approach these deep concerns without caution and careful preparation. (p. 677)

While Noddings was mainly concerned with curricular issues in this article, her words resonated for us. As coaches, we were placing fourth- and fifth-grade students in situations where they could be asked to listen to "more serious" problems, as Deven described earlier. Even though the ten requests written by the end of the school year specified problems with siblings and classmates, we knew there was the *potential* for students to share personal experiences, such as domestic violence or alcohol abuse in the home.

We were faced with a moral dilemma: should we play it safe and back away from giving students the choice to unburden themselves to a peer? Or should we prepare ourselves, the peer helpers, and help seekers by learning how to apply the process to the situation?

The mediation coaches and I decided to work with the peer mediators and prepare a process that would offer students an opportunity to talk about their problems.

Beginning with initial classroom visits, it was important to discuss the options students had when seeking help for problems. They could decide to talk with a caring adult, such as a relative, a current or former teacher, a guidance counselor, or a coach. They might choose to share their problem with someone their own age, such as a friend, a relative, or a peer helper.

Students needed to understand the voluntary nature of their decision to talk with a peer helper, as well as exactly what to expect during a peer helper session. I began by reviewing the introduction, including the promise of confidentiality ("Everything we say here is confidential *except* for information about drugs, alcohol, or weapons on school property and abuse or suicide."). Sharing the request form, follow-up questions, and guidelines (Figures 11.1, 11.2, 11.3) and having peer mediator/helpers present a role play are two ways that I hoped would make the process explicit in the minds of students.

We brainstormed lists of problems that students might bring to a peer helper; this was one way to get students talking about their issues. Scenarios they composed showed a vivid cross section of what a nine- or ten-year-old could want to talk to someone else about:

> Some kids won't let me use the playground equipment.
> Basketball practice keeps me from doing my homework.
> My older brother is skipping school and I'm worried that he's going to get into trouble.
> A kid threatened me if I told about a fight.
> I'm too busy to be a kid.
> My older sister gets to do things I can't.
> People are beating me up for my lunch money.
> My younger sister keeps asking me for help with her homework, and I have trouble getting all of mine done.
> My parents are getting a divorce.
> My mother/father is marrying someone else.
> My cousin died.

It was equally important to devote time to support the peer mediators in their decision to create, implement, and maintain the role of peer helper. What began four years ago as

Hampton Campus School's Peer Mediation Program has grown because of adults' response to students' ideas. Peer helping is a still a new part of our program, and we are still in the process of learning about what it means to students. This year, at least one after-school session a month is devoted exclusively to peer helper role plays and debriefing discussions. That commitment of time may shift, depending on feedback gained from our constant and cooperative pulse taking of Hampton's students. Peer mediator/helpers continue to bring feelings and concerns, as well as insights, to the Issues and Concerns segment during the weekly after-school program (see Figure 10.1).

The peer mediator/helpers can and do choose to talk individually with the coaches. Over the weeks, months, and years, the coaches and peer mediator/helpers have established a sustained and caring relationship based on mutual trust and respect. We take time to listen to each other.

As I reflect on the experience of watching this group of nine- and ten-year-old students create a new role for themselves, certain questions arise that are central to my understanding of issues that emerged:

> Do students perceive needs other than those that are being addressed through the peer mediation program?
>
> What must responsible adults do to prepare students for participation in a helping relationship with their peers?
>
> How are student abilities as flexible thinkers being utilized to maintain, change, or expand the program?
>
> If a peer mediation program aims to prepare students to deal with conflicts peacefully, how can an established program shift into other areas and maintain its integrity?

A Step Back to Reflect

In June, Hampton's new principal, Norman Quinn, and his assistant, Jim Reynolds, met with Diane, Larry, John, and me in Mr. Quinn's office to hear our end-of-year report. One request I made was that fourth- and fifth-grade lunches be scheduled back-to-back. Mr. Quinn looked puzzled and asked, "Why is that?"

"Well, the fifth grades didn't use mediation as much as the fourth grades this year. Because they were scheduled so far apart, I couldn't use fifth-grade mediators in both lunches. So, some mediators are finishing the year without ever having a real mediation."

Mr. Quinn said, "What has this meant to the program?"

"We were worried all year that the mediators would drop out of the program. But they didn't. They wanted to make use of what they have learned as peer mediators to help others. So they've created a new role, peer helper. We used the last four after-school sessions to prepare them. Clare Riley came to one and answered questions about peer counselors or peer helpers. I made arrangements with the fourth- and fifth-grade teachers to visit their classes and explain this new option to students."

Quinn leaned forward and asked, "Is this happening anywhere else?"

"Not to my knowledge," I answered. "But it is consistent with the high degree of caring Hampton students seem capable of showing each other." I had read Bosworth's (1995) article that morning and I shared a quotation I had jotted down from it, "'Programs or strategies that enhance caring values, attitudes, and behaviors by providing students with opportunities to discuss caring, to demonstrate caring to others, and to participate thoughtfully in caring relationships with peers and adults are scarce' [p. 686]. By designing the role of peer helper, Hampton's mediators have found another way to care."

I gave Jim Reynolds and Norman Quinn drafts of a letter home to mediators' parents, which summarized program activities for the year and ended,

> The peer mediators have also created something new for themselves during the past month: the role of peer helper. Any fourth- or fifth-grade student who wants to sit down and talk out a problem can fill out a request and know that a peer helper will listen to his/her situation. A peer helper cannot give advice. However, by using mediator listening and restating skills, a peer helper guides the student to brainstorm ways of dealing with the problem.

As we finished our meeting, Jim Reynolds said he would work on placing the fifth and fourth grades in back-to-back lunch periods. What he did not say was that, because of the State Department of Education Student Learning Time Regulations, he was caught between extending the school day or collapsing the sixty-minute lunch and recess periods into one half hour. In order to comply with the new policy, students would need to eat in fifteen minutes, have recess for fifteen minutes, and return to class. They were to have *even less* time for unstructured social interaction and therefore, even less time to resolve interpersonal and personal problems with the help of peer mediators or peer helpers.

CHAPTER TWELVE

≈ ≈

What's It For?

Make Sure You Wanna Do This

My doctoral research seminar at the University of New Hampshire was taught by Donald Graves (1983, 1994). He is noted for his pioneering efforts in the field of reading and writing instruction; his two decades of research greatly influence the way many teachers approach those subjects today.

Don held the seminar off-campus in his home. He and his wife, Betty, are devoted bird watchers whose wooded lot was hung with feeders. While we sat in the den and talked the talk of researchers, the cardinals, sparrows, tufted titmice, and grosbeaks perched outside and ferreted their preferred seeds from holes in the long feeders, knocking the rest onto the ground for the juncos and mourning doves.

Every once in a while, Don would ask one deceptively simple question: "What's it for?" It seemed to bring us back to earth by making us think about how a theory might function in a particular setting. I apply the question now to a peer mediation program and offer responses that are written from four points of view: administrator, teacher, program coordinator, and peer mediator.

From an Administrator's Perspective

Think back to Danny's story in Chapter 1. It is not difficult to fit his experience into a larger context. Urban-American school violence currently receives intense media coverage and is a problem as complex as Johnny's inability to read was in the 1950s and 1960s. School board members and parents put pressure on school administrators to stanch the flow of blood and return schools to places that are at least demilitarized zones, if not safe havens for learning. While visiting a high school in another state, I observed two solutions to in-school violence: metal detectors and police patrols. Both are dependent upon adults' ability to control students by overpowering them.

Searching for ways to manage school conflict is not just an agenda for administrators from urban settings like Riverton. Johnson et al. (1992) conducted a study in a suburban middle-class elementary school and found that

> After students received the negotiation and mediation training, the student-student conflicts that did occur were by and large managed by the students themselves without the involvement of adults. The frequency of student-student conflicts teachers had to manage dropped 80 percent. The

number of conflicts referred to the principal was reduced to zero. Such a dramatic reduction of referrals of conflicts to adults changed the school discipline program from one that arbitrated conflicts to one that maintained and supported the peer mediation process. (p. 12)

It is hard not to become intrigued and excited by this appealing evidence. Similar claims were made in the December 27, 1995, issue of *MTA Today,* which focused on in-school violence. In an article entitled "Safe Schools: How Can We Keep Them Safe?" an insert featured the following questions: "It seems that conflict resolution classes are gaining in popularity. Do we see this as the answer to violence in school? Do we think every district ought to put this kind of curriculum in place?" The response was impressive:

Conflict resolution that includes . . . peer mediation is the most effective way to reduce or prevent school violence. Conflict resolution involves teaching students how to resolve disagreements nonviolently by working together to arrive at mutually acceptable compromises. Students are taught to settle disputes by going through the process of conflict resolution, which typically includes active listening, acceptance of others' viewpoints, cooperation, and creative problem solving.

In response to the question, "What solutions are working?", *MTA Today* concluded,

Federal support for programs that promote collaboration between parents, communities, and schools to find innovative new approaches for reducing school violence are most successful. A survey of Ohio school districts found that a student peer-mediation program contributed to an average 25 percent reduction in school-safety related suspensions over three years, including a 62 percent reduction in one Dayton middle school. The peer-mediation coordinator of a school in Oakland said mediation is better than suspension, because suspension rarely changes the behavior of students. According to a February 1994 article in the *Wall Street Journal,* there are approximately 5000 peer-mediation programs in the nation's public and private schools and these programs boast an impressive record of success. (p. 19)

MTA Today is the official publication of the Massachusetts Teachers Association; its aim is to stir interest and cause educators to investigate topics further. While supporting MTA's goals, I hope this book has provided a cautionary note to an emerging text full of urgent agendas, multilayered politics, and emotional subtexts. To implement and maintain a peer mediation program in a field that is *in the process of* establishing standards requires a great deal of *care* (Appendixes A.4, A.5, A.6). Implementing and maintaining a peer mediation program is labor-intensive and requires dedicated and well-prepared personnel.

So, what is a peer mediation program for, from an administrator's point of view? To reduce suspensions? To improve school climate (Deutsch 1993; Lam 1989a)? Numbers that reflect fewer office discipline referrals over time seem to be accepted as evidence of success (see Chapter 8, "A Step Back to Reflect"). I noted how that perception was made public during Hampton Campus School's Fourth Induction Ceremony in October 1995. Peer mediators, mediator coaches, parents, students, teachers, and the local press sat in the auditorium and heard congratulatory remarks delivered by the keynote speaker, a presiding justice of the district court. He was followed by Hampton principal Norman Quinn, whose brief speech included the fact that fewer than five Pro-Social Action Reports had been sent home as of that date (see Appendix A.1). He seemed to be making a favorable connection between the presence of a peer mediation program and that statistic.

However, this same evidence could eventually be interpreted as a sign that it is not cost-effective to support a peer mediation program that appears to be no longer necessary. Why *maintain* a program if its "usefulness" seems to have diminished? If there are fewer numbers of office referrals *and* mediations, then is it time to move on to another agenda? Should we expect teachers and coordinators to redirect their organizational energies and high levels of commitment to a different area? In answer I offer another question: What will happen in two to four years when new pairs of feuding Dannys and Jamies sit slumped in Jim Reynolds' office?

Administrators are seeking ways to reduce violence in schools. Yet they must realize that the process, program, or method selected needs to be part of a sustained, connected, and balanced educational experience. A social curriculum, the responsive classroom, and an ethic of care explicitly taught will present students with a connected, ethical worldview. The ideas of Dewey ([1938] 1963, [1916] 1944), Noddings (1984, 1995), Gee (1990), and Charney (1991) can find support in a peer mediation program.

From a Teacher's Perspective

From my experience as a classroom teacher, I saw how the mediation process allowed students to engage in interpersonal problem solving. Fourth-grade mediator Sean Boudreau realized this when he said, "they can use that [experience] another time in a later conflict" (see Chapter 1). It seemed that Sean was able to maximize Vygotsky's (1978) maxim: "What a child can do with assistance today she will be able to do by herself tomorrow" (p. 87). In an important way, students rely on *each other* for a specific kind of assistance and support during the mediation process, which they can use later on their own. I knew that students used language to express their ideas and to examine what they thought they knew. When I became a mediator and program coordinator, three decades in the classroom had taught me the importance of giving peer mediators *time* to talk their way to clarity about the mediation process and the significant ideas it encompasses. *Neutrality. Confidentiality. Voluntariness.*

In a conversation with fourth-grade peer mediator Carrie Gardener, I said that I couldn't schedule mediations during students' instructional time. Her tone took on an incredulous air. "Do they *know* about mediation? Do they know what it's all about? This is one of the main things I learned all year. I learned how to mediate. I learned responsibility, and I helped other people. And we learned what confidential and neutral meant. I didn't know what they meant before this. In the past, if any of my friends got into a fight, I would be in the middle. If I took one person's side, then how would the other one feel? They're both my friends. I've learned those words and how to use them." Throughout this book, I aimed to show how students like Sean and Carrie considered what they were doing to be "learning." They made important connections to themselves and others when they were given time to practice problem finding and solving.

My experience as a classroom teacher helped me to understand how the mediation process fosters functional language use as well. M. A. K. Halliday (1975) identified seven categories of verbal and nonverbal language functions that apply to the ways children learn to communicate. Language used in a single situation may satisfy more than one functional category. "Stop that! You're making me angry" is an example of regulatory language used to control the behavior of others and personal language used to express personal feelings, opinions, and biases.

Halliday maintained that, in order to become proficient language users, children need experience in all seven categories. When I became immersed in mediation's Discourse, I realized that students engaged in a mediation must use *all seven* of Halliday's functions of language to resolve a conflict. I can relate the interdependent mediation process to Halliday's functional categories by using the metaphor of an automobile trip:

1. *Heuristic language* puts the mediators in the driver's seat while the disputants navigate. Mediators use questioning strategies that begin with "What happened?" or "Tell us what brought you to mediation today." They continue to seek information by asking open-ended questions that clarify the conflict and each disputant's needs, as well as by finding out what each disputant is willing to do to solve the problem.
2. *Instrumental language* poses possible destinations for disputants. It is the language used to satisfy disputants' needs and occurs immediately after each disputant tells his/her version of the conflict. The mediator asks, "What do you need to have happen by the end of this mediation?"
3. *Imaginative language* is the spark plug that ignites the mixture of information and creativity as disputants move toward solutions. It is the language used to express creativity. Brainstorming solutions is a key component of mediated agreements. Mediators encourage disputants to work together to come up with as many creative solutions to solving the problem as they possibly can. Analysis and evaluation ("Do you think you can do this by next week?") occurs after multiple solutions are on the table.
4. *Regulatory language* is the language of acceleration and deceleration that mediators use to keep themselves and the disputants on a steady course. Using language to control the behavior of others is basic to the success of the process. It (see Figure 7.2) begins with a set of norms that everyone must hold to (be honest, try to solve the problem, refrain from name-calling and interrupting).
5. *Interactional language* is the language that mediators use not only to ensure a safe and satisfying journey, but also to maintain a future relationship once this trip is completed. It is the language used to establish and maintain social relationships. Mediators are skilled at listening for positive statements from disputants and repeating them in an effort to help rebuild the relationship ("Joey says that you have been his good friend since second grade.")
6. *Personal language* connects all participants on the journey. This is the lan-

guage used to express personal opinions, feelings, and biases ("I'm upset because every time I go to my seat, I look over and she is whispering to Dana about me.") Mediators develop an awareness of the difference between disputants' statements of fact or opinion and rephrase and reframe issues: "Let me see if I understood what you just said. You feel upset when you think someone is saying things about you."

7. *Informative language* is the fuel that keeps the mediation going. It is the language used to transmit information throughout the process. Mediators and disputants are involved in defining and processing issues and sorting and conveying information that could lead to a resolution.

In her middle school study, Bosworth (1995) observed "that most interactions between students or between students and their teachers were neutral. Each went about his or her business without engaging in overt acts of caring or uncaring. Mostly they were pleasant and polite to one another, but the structure of the school day left little space or time for interpersonal interaction" (p. 689).

So, what's a peer mediation program for, from a teacher's perspective? If students are going to use language functionally and meaningfully in school, then they must use it in situations that are authentic and socially driven. Students are able to move through the mediation process while keeping goals in sight and understanding consequences of decisions and agreements they make. Peer mediation programs and conflict management skills are vehicles that will last students through a lifetime of problem solving (Davis and Porter 1985b).

From a Program Coordinator's Perspective

In April 1995, I tore open a letter from Kelly Felenzo, one of Hampton's first mediators. With two years of experience as a fourth- and fifth-grade mediator, she moved on to the middle school. Unfortunately, staffing constraints there meant that the program served only the upper grades:

> Well, I'm sort of in mediation. I signed up for it, but they never had a training. I guess it seems as if we [sixth-grade students] don't need it because by now most people shrug the names off their backs. Rumors, threats, and any violence go directly to Mr. DiGregorio.

Kelly seemed to be critical of the status quo because she had dealt with conflicts in school in another way. She continued: "We had the 'Up With People' exchange students come to our school, and we had a big circle discussion about how all people are created equal. It really reminded me of how we used to talk on Thursday afternoons and just run out of time." I read this as an affirmation of the time devoted to acquiring mediation's Discourse during our weekly after-school program when problem finding and solving, caring, and thoughtfulness were the agenda.

Kelly showed her sense of pride in being a part of the new program and shared my feeling about the fact that peer mediation programs were spreading to other schools in Riverton: "I looked back at the newspaper article with the picture of Ricky and Amber doing the role play. I think that mediation is kind of contagious because we were the first [in the city] and all the schools started it, which is nice. But the fact is that we all made it happen."

Rexford Brown (1991) stated,

> The primary conditions for thoughtfulness—mystery, uncertainty, disagreement, important questions, ambiguity, curiosity—exist in every classroom. You see them in the faces of the children; you hear them in the halls. Potential learning opportunities are everywhere, but these fertile conditions are either ignored or perceived as barriers to teaching, as threats to order.
>
> If you want to change individuals, you usually have to make them conscious of things that are right in front of their faces, things that they cannot see while everyone else can. You often have to help them learn how to listen to themselves, how to recognize contradictions in what they are saying, patterns of expression that reveal underlying assumptions and ideas. So it is with changing organizational cultures: you start with language. (p. 234)
>
> [Brown and his team of researchers] asked teachers and administrators what they saw as the principal constraints on giving students more opportunities to think, solve problems, and learn to use their minds more effectively . . . *The most frequently given reason for not moving toward an instruction more conducive to thoughtfulness was time.* (p. 235)

Students need time to mediate their disputes. During the 1995–96 school year, students' lunch *and* recess were collapsed into thirty minutes. There have been very few mediations over the first four months of school, and this is part of a schoolwide trend. The reduced number of requests, mediations, and agreements should not necessarily be interpreted as a sign of diminishing need. At first, some students at Hampton tested the waters by making up conflicts or by bringing conflicts they could have easily solved themselves to mediation. Although the novelty of mediation has worn off, student conflicts remain woven into the fabric of school life. By maintaining a conflict resolution curriculum, using problem finding and solving as a cross-curricular framework, students can work their way through most everyday disputes. However, peer mediation should still be available "if all else fails"—if a problem is so knotty and tangled that a neutral third-person team can help to identify underlying issues and help to sort out who will do what in a written agreement. Students attending a school with a peer mediation program have joined a Discourse community in which they practice talking, listening, reading, and writing grounded in mediation's belief system. Moreover, maintaining a program sends a message to everyone: having students solve their own interpersonal problems is a priority in this school.

What's a peer mediation program for, from a coordinator's point of view? The experience of writing this book has helped me to think about it in this way: when students choose to fill out a peer mediation request and are given time and a place to sit down with peers who are prepared to help them deal with their issues, each is participating in an overt act of thoughtfulness and caring. I believe that it is an experience that we, who control much of their school lives, must offer to students.

From a Peer Mediator's Perspective

Early drafts of this chapter presented a different sequence—the peer mediators were first and foremost in my mind, while the adults came after. When I told my husband, John, how I was structuring it, he said, "It should be the other way around. End the book with the peer mediators' voices. It's their book. Let their words be the last to be remembered." I believe he was right.

This final section is a composite of several interviews. Over a week's time in June 1995, I gathered small groups of peer mediators in a private space near my office, and we talked about the program. I told them I was writing this book and asked, "What would you like to tell adults who are interested in peer mediation?" Their responses were filled with the wisdom of practice. They discussed what they considered important about their experience—what they learned and what they needed and expected from their parents, teachers, and mediation coaches. The tape recorder whirred quietly on the table behind our circle of chairs.

> *Judith Parker:* I thought that being a mediator gave me responsibility because I had to go on duty and keep my cool. If there's a person in mediation being terrible, you can't just yell. You have to be like a waitress. You have to take it. And that helped me with my temper. I had a bad temper. Once in a follow-up [see Figure 7.5], the disputant wasn't being cooperative. It made me angry. If that happened before, I would have wound up screaming at the person. But now I think about what to say.
>
> *Renee Mallory:* I think mediation is good because it's a good way to discipline yourself. It's a good way to do, like Miss Riley, says, "Use your words, not your hands." Instead of going up to a person and, saying, "Hey, I heard about this rumor," and punching him out, it's a good way to talk about it. It helps you realize that what you *want to do* might not be the right thing. It helped me to realize that I have to think about what I'm going to say before I say it and think about what I'm going to do before I do it.
>
> My brother always takes my perfume and sprays it everywhere. I took him outside and said, "Sammy, I really don't like it when you take my perfume because it's expensive." He said, "I'm sorry," and we shook and went in. It helped.
>
> *Eleanor Santoro:* My sister was turning up MTV really loud, and I was trying to take a nap. So I started yelling and then, my mom calmed us down. We talked and ended up compromising. I took my nap in the other room and she ended up turning it down a little bit, so it worked out.
>
> *Renee:* My parents were arguing and I said, "Do a mediation or something. Don't yell. Talk." Like they were fighting over where we were going to go on our vacation. I said, "Call the other people who are going with us and figure it out with them. Don't yell and scream at each other."
>
> I was afraid that they were going to say, "Don't interrupt!" or that my dad would say, "I'm your father!" But he kind of looked at me, then they sat down and started to talk to each other. It was really weird.
>
> *Andy Scranton:* When my father starts getting mad and yelling at my brother, I think he's giving a bad example. I'm not saying that my brother is

right, but it gives him the courage to be more aggressive when he's mad.

Renee [agreeing]: My little brothers look up to my dad and sometimes he swears. Because they're younger, they pick up that swear and say it. My dad has to correct himself. "I can't say that around the kids." I bet you that all grown-ups swear at some point. You have to learn to be less aggressive around the kids. The kids pick it up and as they grow older, they will think that is the way to act all their life. It's like a chain reaction. This kid follows dad and if the kid is popular, other kids will follow him.

Bob Lincoln: I'd tell grown-ups to take the advice we give to each other: Use your words, not physical violence. Some people are in jail for beating up other grown-ups and putting them into the hospital. It's not good . . . the killing and violence.

We stopped talking for a minute. Then Eleanor summed up by saying, "It's really important for adults to do the right thing."

Pam Bonneau [opening another discussion]: I once had a mediation where disputants were forced by the teacher to go to mediation. The teacher said to the kids, "Well, you two are going to mediation at lunch." Teachers sometimes *want you* to do mediation and maybe you don't want to. And you can't say no to a teacher.

Some students get into trouble and their teachers see them go to mediation. One of them comes back to class and the teacher says, "I see you went to mediation. Wise choice." That could put pressure on the kid.

Deven Mancini: Some teachers don't understand mediation. They should get together, kind of like we're doing now in this group, and talk about it.

Hilary Comeau: Some kids get all mad because we were getting all the attention, like teacher's pet.

Carrie Gardener: And we don't want a reputation like that. I say that people might drop out because of that pressure.

Allison Dominico: Kids could interview kids about the program. Or do a survey every once in a while. You could tell them, "Whatever you suggest, we'll consider it. We'll use your ideas to make the program better for you."

Clara Binette: If I could give advice to grown-ups, it would be to make sure you *wanna* do this. In one year, they want to start this program and after a while they want to stop it. Make sure you stay "into it." Lots of kids want to join up and then if the leader quits, then they can't have it anymore. Make a commitment.

Willie Fenton [passionately]: Kids are important, and we need a leader.

Amanda Terry: Adults have to really believe in mediation themselves. They can't only do it for a job. They have to do it at home, too. They have to make a commitment to it because the peer mediators follow in their footsteps. If they can say, "Well, my leader quit when I was in elementary school, so why can't I?"

Carrie: And one thing about the adult volunteers who are in the program. They should be dependable. Like if they're scheduled to be on duty with us, they should come.

Erica Kenevian: I'd say to use your common sense and be organized so if you want to start a program, you'll know when and where to make things happen and when and where to put things. Before you first start the program, think about all the things you will have to do to get it going. And don't get frustrated and quit. It might work out. Don't put an end to it.

If a school doesn't have a program, the kids think the adults are the ones who can solve their problems. With a program, the kids don't count on the adults, but on themselves.

As I sit at my word processor reading the words of these fourth- and fifth-grade students, I recognize a feeling that has overcome me many times in the past few years. I am intensely proud to have been in the company of such good people. There is one passage spoken by Clara that I find myself replaying because it sounds so characteristically true to her and other peer mediators' way of seeing themselves in the world. "Sometimes kids tease me about being a peer mediator—kids from other schools around my neighborhood." When I asked her how they knew she was a mediator, she said,

Because I tell them. I talk about being a mediator. I'm proud of being a mediator. I went through two days of training and come once a week after school. Sometimes it was just boring, but I stuck with it. I wonder sometimes, "Why am I doing this?" but two minutes later, I know I'm doing this because I want to make a difference in the way the future generation acts. If the kids at Hampton and other schools start acting different, this future generation will look a lot brighter.

APPENDIX A.1

≈ ≈

Pro-Social Action Report

Dear Parent:
   Please sign and have your child return to the office.

_____
PARENT SIGNATURE

Date: _____ Time: _____
Student(s): _____ Homeroom Teacher: _____
Referred by: _____
Place: _____
Administrator: _____

SITUATION: (What happened? Where did it happen? Who said and did what? What facts are agreed upon by all parties?)

PROBLEM(S): (What is the problem? How did each person feel about the problem? The problem statement is to be agreed upon by all parties.)

SOLUTION(S): (What will each person do about this problem? How will each avoid the situation another time? What have you learned from this situation?)

CONSEQUENCE(S): (The consequences should relate to the problem and are to be agreed upon by the adult and student[s]. There may be different consequences for each student.)

Parent comment:
_____
_____
_____

Teacher comment:
_____
_____
_____

APPENDIX A.2

≈ ≈

Annotated Bibliography of Program Resources

In the search for books and materials to support the range of concepts, topics, and skills that come under the heading "conflict resolution" and "peer mediation," look first to your own preparation in the role of program coordinator, coach, or volunteer (see Appendixes A.4 and A.5). Ask yourself how you came to understand the role of mediator and which methods (readings, discussions, role plays, videos, and activities) worked to help you learn what it means to take on this responsibility. As a mediator/coordinator/coach, you must first *learn about the school's and community's cultures* (see Chapters 2 and 3).

Learning theory and research point to the need for teachers to build on the richness and complexity of students' prior knowledge and experiences. So it will be with teaching students conflict resolution strategies and the mediation process. You will find yourself gathering and creating your own materials, as well as purchasing them.

Should you join the National Association for Mediation in Education/National Institute for Dispute Resolution (NAME/NIDR; see Appendix A.6)? Yes. One of your most valuable resources could be their annual Directory of Members. It makes sense to seek out people who have had firsthand experience with peer mediation programs. One of my goals in writing this book was to share my experience—I hope that you have learned from it.

You will also receive NAME/NIDR's annotated catalog as part of your membership. Part of their function has been to act as a central clearinghouse for program books and materials. Be aware of the expanding interest in mediation with its attendant proliferation of books and materials. The more you read, the more you will appreciate the differences among program models and the better you will be able to weigh differences with respect to your own program.

The information given here is by no means an exhaustive look at resources, but I offer samples from several *categories* of books and materials that continue to be useful to me.

Theory and Research

A comprehensive trio of books from Jossey-Bass Publishers (San Francisco) offers readers a look at mediation theory, research, and practice through essays and interviews with leaders in the field of mediation:

Bush, R. A. B., and J. P. Folger. 1994. *The Promise of Mediation: Responding to Conflict Through Empowerment and Recognition.*

Kolb, D., and Associates. 1994. *When Talk Works.*

Bunker, B. B., J. Z. Rubin, and Associates. 1995. *Conflict, Cooperation, and Justice: Essays Inspired by the Work of Morton Deutsch.*

Conflict Resolution and Peer Mediation Curricula

Sadalla, G., M. Holmberg, and J. Halligan. 1990. *Conflict Resolution: An Elementary School Curriculum.* San Francisco, CA: The Community Board Program, Inc. This curriculum provides a bridge between conflict resolution and peer mediation because it gives students experience with strategies necessary to understanding and using both: communicating clearly, expressing feelings appropriately, listening actively, identifying conflict, and appreciating cultural differences (see Chapter 2 for an explanation of these strategies). I found the last chapter of the curriculum on peer mediation to be both practical and deceptively simple. Its lessons can be used to teach all students what will happen during mediation so that they will be well prepared when they voluntarily enter into the process with a pair of neutral third parties to resolve a conflict. I have also used the activities for the initial training of peer mediators. While another section provides a description of "Students as Conflict Managers for Their Peers," it seems to underestimate the amount of preparation and work required on the part of adults interested in implementing and sustaining a peer mediation program.

Sadalla, G., M. Henriquez, and M. Holmberg. 1987. *Conflict Resolution: A Secondary Curriculum.* San Francisco, CA: The Community Board Program, Inc. This work aims to involve students in grades 7–12 in conflict resolution through readings, discussion groups, and activities.

Kreidler, W. J. 1990. *Elementary Perspectives 1: Teaching Concepts of Peace and Conflict.* Cambridge, MA: Educators for Social Responsibility.

———. 1984. *Creative Conflict Resolution: More Than 200 Activities for Keeping Peace in the Classroom.* Glenview, IL: GoodYear Books. William Kreidler offers elementary classroom teachers, guidance counselors, and mediation coaches specific interdisciplinary lessons that involve students in the active learning necessary to build their experiences with conflict resolution.

Information-Program Awareness

An ongoing task for any mediation program coordinator is to educate the school and community population. For example, NAME Publications produces a general packet, *Rationale for Starting a Program,* containing articles from journals and magazines that teach about mediation and conflict resolution in schools. The collection represents views from several perspectives (administrators, program directors, and educational leaders) suitable for sharing with parents, faculty, and members of the community.

Peer Mediation Program Materials

Cohen, R. 1995. *Students Resolving Conflict: Peer Mediation in Schools.* Glenview, IL: GoodYear Books. Cohen, an expert in the area of in-school mediation, says something in his preface that I believe cannot be said too many times:

> Please be advised that *Students Resolving Conflict* is not designed to teach you how to mediate or how to train students to mediate. No book alone can accomplish this task. The best way to learn how to mediate is to participate in a qualified training program that includes extensive super-

vised practice. This book should be used to supplement such a mediation training program. (p. v)

Cohen's book is a complete and practical guide to implementing a peer mediation program at middle and high school levels. He offers detailed lists of "shoulds" with respect to how best to design a program that fits the needs of your school. Cohen cites a range of issues and concerns that are certain to emerge once you begin to explore the possibility of bringing a peer mediation program into a school's culture. He also explains what to look for as a program becomes established. It is an objective and thorough look at "the big picture," a necessary resource for anyone seeking to start up a program or examine an existing one.

After initial training, maintaining a meaningful, ongoing training program for peer mediators is a special challenge for coordinators and coaches. Once the program is under way, it is important to observe how various aspects are working. For example, a coordinator might notice that some of the agreements need to be more specific or that conflict summaries need to be less specific. Ongoing training (our weekly after-school program) gives the time to refine certain skills, as well as the opportunity to debrief. The following books and materials are useful in preparing for ongoing training activities:

Schrumpf, F., D. Crawford, and H. C. Usadel. 1991. *Peer Mediation: Conflict Resolution in Schools Program Guide.* Champaign, IL: Research Press.

Aetna Life Insurance Company. 1993. *Resolving Conflict Through Mediation: An Educational Program for Middle School Students.* Hartford, CT: Developed by Aetna Life Insurance Company.

Johnson, D. W., and R. T. Johnson. 1991. *Teaching Children to Be Peacemakers.* Edina, MN: Interaction Book.

Schmidt, F., A. Friedman, and J. Marvel. 1992. *Mediation for Kids: Kids in Dispute Settlement.* Miami Beach, FL: Grace Contrino Abrams Peace Foundation, Inc.

APPENDIX A.3

≈ ≈

Community Program Brochure

What Is Mediation?

Mediation is a process which allows two parties to come before a neutral third party, the mediator, in hopes of finding a mutually satisfactory agreement.

What Do Mediators Do?

A mediator helps people involved in a dispute explore ways of resolving a problem by listening, guiding discussion, clarifying legal and emotional issues, setting the agenda, and writing agreements.

What Are the Advantages of Mediation?

All decisions about the outcome are made by the people involved and the solutions are often a Win-Win situation. Mediation is a quick, convenient, and nonconfrontational process. Consult with the Mediation Office or with your attorney to see if your case is appropriate for mediation.

Who Are the Mediators?

The mediators are community volunteers who have been trained and certified by ———.

How Do I Request Mediation?

Court Referrals

In Small Claims matters, check off the "Mediation" box in Part 5 of your complaint form when you file at the courthouse. The Mediation Office will contact you to schedule a mediation.

Small Claim mediations are held on Mondays and Tuesdays from 9:00–3:00 and on evenings or Saturdays by special arrangement.

Minor Criminal complaints such as disturbing the peace, trespassing, assault and battery, are referred to the Mediation Office by the Clerk-Magistrate. You may indicate your willingness to mediate these disputes to the Clerk-Magistrate when you file your complaint or at your Show-Cause hearing. Mediations of this type of complaint will be scheduled only at the request of the Clerk-Magistrate.

Mediations can be arranged in *Eviction* cases and *Landlord-Tenant* disputes by phoning the Mediation Office before the trial date or by approaching the mediator at the courthouse on the day of the trial.

Community Referrals

——— also provides mediation at the request of area residents. If you would like to settle parent-child difficulties over children's curfews, chores, or school attendance, work, and behavior or neighborhood disputes over noise, friends, parking, visitors, etc. You should phone or write to the Mediation Office to discuss the matter with a Mediation Coordinator.

———— also takes referrals from the Department of Social Services and from Probation Officers.

What if We Don't Settle?

If no agreement is reached, the case is sent back to the court and will be heard before a judge. Recourse to trial is never forfeited by participation in mediation.

What About Agreements?

In Small Claims and Eviction cases the agreement becomes a court judgment. In minor criminal cases and community referrals it is a good faith agreement between the disputing parties.

Fee Schedule

The following is an outline of the basic fee schedule in effect for ———— Mediation programs.

Please note that the private mediation fees include a nonrefundable administrative fee charged to the party initiating the mediation and a flat fee for an initial session of up to two hours. There is no fee charged for the time spent by coordinators and mediators in *preparation* for the first session or for preparation and document review time beyond the first session.

Court Mediation: Small claims, minor criminal, eviction, and housing cases where application for court process has already been filed.   No fee

Monitoring Service: Offered to parties who desire that their agreements be supervised by ————. Monitoring includes communication between parties needed to insure that the terms of the agreement are held to. The Mediation Office acts as a conduit for transfer of payments between parties. The office receives and forwards payments, maintains records, and acts as a liaison to the court. $25.00

Private Mediation: Mediation requested in business, community, family, neighborhood disputes.

Administrative fee	$10.00
Initial session	$100.00
(split among parties)	
Each additional hour	$50.00
(split among parties)	

No one is refused mediation on the basis of inability to pay. Phone the Mediation Office for information on a sliding fee scale.

APPENDIX A.4

≈ ≈

MAMPP Mediation Training Standards

Reprinted by Permission of Massachusetts Association of Mediation Programs and Practitioners, 133 Federal Street, 11th Floor, Boston, MA 02110

Statement of Purpose

The Massachusetts Association of Mediation Programs and Practitioners (MAMPP) is an organization of mediators, mediation programs, and others whose purpose is to promote, support, and develop the use of mediation to resolve disputes throughout the Commonwealth. We are committed to the use of trained community mediators to provide readily accessible mediation services.

MAMPP has established Mediation Training Standards to provide all community mediation programs, mediation trainers, and mediators with clear guidelines outlining minimum standards for the development and ongoing education of community mediators. Included are basic training, apprenticeship, and continuing education guidelines; guidelines for mediation trainers; and fundamental qualities of successful mediators.

The Mediation Training Standards have also been established to provide an assurance of quality to consumers, referral services, judges, funders, and policymakers. The Massachusetts Association of Mediation Programs and Practitioners recommends that all community mediator programs and mediator trainers uphold the training standards in all aspects of their work in developing and supporting community mediators to practice in Massachusetts.

I. Basic Mediation Training and Apprenticeship

Philosophy: Basic mediation training emphasizes interactive participation, encouraging "learning by doing" in a constructive and supportive atmosphere. It includes a mixture of theory and practice that enhances the performance of trainees and provides a variety of learning techniques that reflects a sensitivity to individual learning styles. Lecture and role-play content covers basic considerations in the types of disputes addressed by the mediation program. A mediation apprenticeship allows the trainer to demonstrate his/her competency to integrate the lessons from training into actual practice. Evaluation is based primarily on competency as demonstrated in coached role-plays and actual mediations.

A. Training Format
    1. Basic training
        a. minimum of thirty hours; thirty-six to forty hours recommended
        b. minimum of three coached role-plays with trainee as mediator, including a minimum of one complete role-play (introduction to conclusion of session)

    c. one coach for each small group during role-play (a maximum of six trainees)

  2. Apprenticeship

    a. follows successful completion of a minimum of thirty hours of basic training

    b. offers complexity appropriate to general skill level of newly trained mediator

    c. includes performing a minimum of one actual mediation, with or observed by a skilled mediator who will conduct a debriefing session with the apprentice and provide the program with an evaluation of the apprentice's competency

    d. includes observing a minimum of one actual mediation conducted by a skilled mediator who will conduct a debriefing session with the apprentice

  3. Evaluation

    a. includes explicit criteria for successful completion of basic training and apprenticeship

    b. final evaluation of trainee's performance in basic training and apprenticeship must be conveyed to trainee no later than one year after basic training ends

    c. schedule of evaluations

      1) assessment of trainee by self and training team

        a) during and/or directly following each role-play

        b) midpoint of basic training

        c) conclusion of basic training

        d) conclusion of apprenticeship

      2) assessment of trainer(s) by trainees at conclusion of basic training

      3) assessment of training by trainees

        a) midpoint of basic training

        b) conclusion of basic training

B. Components of Basic Training

  1. Lecture/discussion/exercise

    a. Overview of program

      1) Explanation of training, apprenticeship, and evaluation format

      2) Role of program

      3) MAMPP Standards of Practice

    b. Overview of ADR

      1) ADR processes

      2) Nature of conflict/behaviors in conflict

      3) Steps of mediation process

      4) Role of mediator

    c. Mediation skills

      1) Listening

      2) Neutral language

      3) Rephrasing

      4) Asking follow-up questions

      5) Reframing
      6) Summarizing
      7) Identifying issues
      8) Barriers to agreement
      9) Negotiating agreement
      10) Notetaking
      11) Agreement writing
    d. Critical issues
      1) Values, bias awareness
      2) Personally sensitive issues
      3) Critical issues: physical/substance abuse, power imbalance
      4) Cultural diversity
      5) Dilemmas for the mediator
  2. Mediation demonstration
  3. Coached role-plays
    Observation and critique of mediator conduct as outlined under Mediator Conduct.

II. Continuing Education

Philosophy: In order to retain and enhance the skills required to serve people through mediation, ongoing training is necessary.

A. Training Format
Minimum of two sessions or six hours per year, session within six months of completion of basic training.

B. Approved Continuing Education Opportunities
  1. Any advanced training offered by MAMPP community mediation programs
  2. Any training or workshop offered by:
    Academy of Family Mediators (AFM)
    American Arbitration Association (AAA)
    Educators for Social Responsibility (ESR)
    Harvard Program of Negotiation (PON)
    Massachusetts Association of Mediation Programs (MAMPP)
    Massachusetts Council on Family Mediation, Inc. (MCFM)
    National Association of Mediation in Education (NAME)
    National Conference of Peacemaking and Conflict Resolution (NCPCR)
    National Institute of Dispute Resolution (NIDR)
    Society of Professionals in Dispute Resolution (SPIDR)
    Violence Prevention Project (VPP)
  3. Any academic course in Alternative Dispute Resolution (ADR)
  4. Training approved by local MAMPP community mediation program, including academic courses and workshops in related fields, when relevant to mediation (i.e. law, social work, psychology)
  5. Internships with mediation organizations that enhance a mediator's skills beyond what is required for initial competency; approved by local MAMPP program director
  6. Observation of experienced mediator, followed by debriefing session

III. Mediation Trainers: Qualities and Responsibilities

Philosophy: The process of helping people improve their interpersonal and facilitative skills as mediators is an intimate one; it requires a trainee to demonstrate a willingness to take risks, perform publicly and receive critical coaching and an effective mediation trainer to be sensitive to each trainee's needs and individual learning style and pace. The mediation trainer should have extensive experience as a mediator in order to be accepted as a credible teacher and role model. Thorough knowledge of the mediation process and a mediator's techniques and strategic choices is also essential. Teaching skills that a trainer requires include flexibility concerning approach, a lively stage presence, effective presentation skills, an ability to promote positive group dynamics among learners and a sense of the developmental nature of skills acquisition.

A. *Background Requirements*
  1. Training and experience as mediator, as outlined in Basic Training, Apprenticeship, and Continuing Education sections
  2. Commitment to upholding MAMPP's Training Standards and Standards of Practice
  3. Proficiency in all areas outlined in Training Requirements

B. *Training Requirements*
  1. Designing the training
     The trainer:
     a. is able to create a realistic, logical agenda
     b. has a thorough knowledge of the materials to be covered
     c. selects and/or develops materials to be used in training
     d. consults with other members of the training team in order to deliver a consistent approach
  2. Training mediator candidates
     The trainer:
     a. is organized and professional in all aspects of conduct
     b. creates a comfortable learning environment that encourages risk-taking
     c. is committed to the growth of individual candidates
     d. transmits concepts clearly
     e. effectively coaches candidates during role-playing
     f. maintains the morale and momentum of group
     g. revises format as needed
     h. provides constructive feedback to candidates and co-trainers
     i. equally distributes opportunities for trainees to learn by applying skills
  3. Assessing mediator candidates
     The trainer:
     a. evaluates performance of candidates midway through training, at conclusion of basic training, and conclusion of apprenticeship
     b. delivers evaluations clearly to candidates
     c. assesses overall training and makes recommendations for improvement to training coordinator
     d. exchanges evaluative comments with other trainers regarding trainer performances in order to improve the state of the art

     e. provides program director with a written summary assessment of each candidate

IV. Mediator Conduct

Philosophy: Mediators have an obligation to the public and the profession to conduct their practice in a competent and ethical manner. Central to the code of behavior required of mediators is a commitment to and respect for the parties and the mediation process. Central also is the personal integrity with which each mediator enhances the quality of the process. The following list of observable behaviors is not intended as an exhaustive list, but as the minimum requirement for basic mediator competency.

A. Managing the Process
The mediator:
1. is able to explain the mediation process and role of mediator
2. sets a tone that helps to put people at ease
3. guides transitions between stages
4. has a good sense of timing
5. is flexible in tailoring the process to the needs of the parties
6. respects the parties' rights to make their own decisions
7. upholds the parameters of confidentiality

B. Managing Interactions
The mediator:
1. maintains an open, honest and supportive atmosphere
2. treats parties with respect and affirmation
3. maintains neutrality
4. demonstrates effective active listening skills
5. uses clear language
6. maintains composure when challenged
7. avoids appearance of bias or favoritism
8. handles conflict and strong emotions effectively
9. helps parties to see things positively
10. helps parties to see problems from the others' point of view
11. is able to ask tough questions in a nonthreatening manner
12. avoids asking leading questions, giving opinions, or making judgments
13. works cooperatively with co-mediator
14. keeps discussions focused on issues relevant to the negotiations
15. demonstrates patience and persistence

C. Managing Information
The mediator:
1. asks relevant and open-ended questions
2. presents and reframes information clearly
3. seeks understanding and underlying needs
4. determines areas of flexibility
5. keeps track of new information and changing perspectives
6. develops strategic direction
7. introduces brainstorming or role reversal to encourage re-evaluation of positions and development of options

8. encourages parties to develop new solutions
9. identifies common interests
10. encourages collaborative efforts between parties
11. recognizes potential areas of agreement
12. summarizes at appropriate times
13. supports parties' control of the outcome
14. helps to frame a clear, balanced, specific, and future-oriented agreement

APPENDIX A.5

≈ ≈

Recommended Standards for School-Based Mediation Programs

Reprinted by Permission of National Association for Mediation in Education/National Institute for Dispute Resolution, 1726 M Street, NW, Suite 500, Washington, DC 20036-4502

I. Rationale

As the field of conflict resolution in education has grown dramatically over the past ten years, so has the proliferation of programs across the country and around the world. It is the role of NAME, as the international professional organization in the field, to provide both leadership and guidance for these programs. The questions of standards for school programs began to surface in the late 1980s, and an ad hoc committee was set up to begin the study of this issue in the early 1990s.

The standards presented here represent the work of the committee and the membership and are meant to ensure quality and to stimulate thought within peer mediation programs. These standards are meant to be reviewed every three years to ensure that they are relevant, flexible, and current.

II. Glossary

Program coordinator: Person who coordinates the daily operations of a peer mediation program

Level I trainer: One who trains students and staff in a peer mediation program

Level II trainer: One who trains a Level I trainer

Level III trainer: One who trains the Level I and/or Level II trainers as well as undertakes an advisory or supervisory role with them

III. School Assessment and Commitment to a Peer Mediation Program

A. Assessment

Assessment of the school is a very important part of the process. This can be done in one of two ways.

1. Talk with the administration and faculty. Find out what a school assumes about a peer mediation program. Define the needs of the school and what a peer mediation program can and cannot do for them. Clear and realistic expectations for the effectiveness of the program must be set in advance.
2. Do a formal inventory assessment, which might include interviews, surveys, and focus groups, done over at least a week's time.

B. Initial Commitment and Subsequent Program Support

In order for a Peer Mediation program to be really successful, it is necessary that the whole school community both understands the program and its principles and commits to supporting them. Also, research shows that if administrators support the program, it's much more likely to succeed. Below are sample strategies and activities that school leaders could use toward accomplishing this goal.

1. Presentations by those who are to do the training *before* the decision is made to adopt the program should be made to relevant school communities, such as faculty, students, parents, etc. Before the school commits to undertaking a Peer Mediation program, it is suggested that the faculty actively come to an agreement to undertake and support the program. This commitment will help ensure their cooperation with those who are managing the program.
2. After this commitment has been made, training sessions in conflict resolution, mediation, and bias awareness should be offered to the administrators, coordinators, staff, students and/or parent groups.
3. Skits and demonstrations of the mediation process should be presented at student, faculty, and parent gatherings throughout the year, showing a variety of ways this concept can be used both in school and home situations.
4. Also, it is strongly suggested that a conflict resolution curriculum be developed for the whole school as soon as possible.

IV. Coordinators Training

Program Coordinators are responsible for administering and maintaining the peer mediation program. Support for and coordination of the program is essential.

A. Program Coordinator Training
The training includes the following:
1. Introductory mediation training skills
2. Role of mediation in the school. Mediation is a process separate from that of counseling or discipline.
3. Benefits of a mediation program in school
4. Step-by-step guide of program set-up
5. How to select students
6. How to select materials for training
7. How to bring faculty on board
8. How to inform the student body
9. Problem-solving
10. A variety of models to help tailor the program to the needs of the school
11. Options for scheduling
12. Ideas for program maintenance
13. The role of students in program maintenance
14. Opportunities for further training for staff coordinators
15. Resources and services available to support the program

B. As many members of the coordinating team as possible should attend the student training.

V. Training of Program Coordinators as Level I Trainers

A. Prerequisites
1. Coordinator training
2. Attend student mediator training

3. Experience as a coordinator—if not experienced, access to a Level III trainer or program coordinator would be invaluable.

B. Content of Training

It is important that the content of training for Level I trainers be in agreement with the model established for student mediator training.

1. Review of basic training information and mediation process for personal application and for training students
2. Trainer skills and strategies to be mastered
   a. How to follow the process of conducting a student training
   b. Skills essential to mediation and how to impart those skills to students

C. Training Techniques/Methods

1. Examination and use of a variety of exercises
2. Role-plays
3. Coaching skills
4. Lecture—when and how much
5. Facilitation of groups
6. Brainstorming
7. Demonstrations
8. Video

May add a note about trainers need for open-mindedness toward student, process, and program.

D. Materials

Since there is a variety of manuals and other materials in the field, it is important that coordinators have the opportunity to see several different ones to enhance the quality of their program and approaches.

E. Length of Training

1. Coordinator training: minimum 6 hours
2. Level I training: 14–30 hours

F. Some Concerns to Be Discussed in Level I Training

1. Mediation experience: It is important that those who are training students to be mediators have actual mediation experience themselves.
2. Ways in which Level I trainers can increase the skill level of the school community in the resolution of conflict

VI. Requirements for Level II Trainers

A. Level II Trainer Must:

- Have taken a formal Basic adult mediation course (min. 20 hours)
- Have mediated at least five (ten) cases
- Have monitored or run a school program for at least two years
- Have apprenticed and/or trained with experienced Level III trainer (see VII below)
- Have networked with other trainers and professionals in the field
- Have taken at least one advanced course in peer mediation, conflict resolution, or adult mediation (see B below)
- Is acknowledged by peers as an effective and experienced trainer (see C below)

B. Advanced Trainings

The topics include but are not limited to:

- Multicultural issues
- Bias awareness
- The various models of peer mediation programs
- Funding
- Special problems and issues in mediation
- Problem-solving
- Conflict resolution theory
- Program administration and planning
- Systems-design for schools
- Classroom management
- Negotiation

C. Evaluation of Trainers

- By Level III trainer
- By participants (students, parents, staff)
- Self-evaluation and responding to above evaluations
- Peer evaluation

VII. Requirements for Level III Trainers

A. Level III Trainer Must:

- Have broad knowledge of the field of mediation, peer mediation, and conflict resolution
- Meet all the requirements for a Level I and II trainer
- Have been working full-time in the field of peer mediation for a minimum of two years
- Have attended and presented training courses, conferences, and workshops in the field
- Have read and used various models of the peer mediation trainings
- Have developed her/his own program after studying various programs
- Have tested and used the above training in at least ten settings
- Have personally designed and implemented a peer mediation program in a school, agency, or other youth setting
- Have run or supported this program throughout a full year to discover and work with its strengths and weaknesses
- Be willing to give time to apprentices to discuss strengths and weaknesses during the training and also be available to give support once the new trainer is training

VIII. Preparation of Student Mediators

A. Content

Respect for difference and multicultural issues is a necessary part of the preparation of student mediators. This can be accomplished by using role-plays and activities that deal with cross cultural issues. The following content areas are included in mediation trainings:

1. Conflict
   a. What is conflict? How can we learn from it?

    b. Conflict resolution styles (flight, denial, cooperative problem-solving, fight-confrontation)

    c. Types of conflict (property disputes, rumors, put-downs, values, relationships, etc.)

  2. Communication

    a. Why it is important, nonverbal communication, good and poor listening

    b. Paraphrasing

    c. Active listening (restating, summarizing, clarifying, reflecting, encouraging, listening for feelings)

    d. Open-ended questions, neutral language

    e. "I" Messages

  3. Mediation

    a. Definition

    b. Preliminary assumptions (voluntary participation, confidentiality, etc.)

    c. Ground rules (no interrupting, no put-downs, agree to solve the problem)

    d. Steps/stages of mediation

    e. Points of view (perceptions, positions, and interests)

    f. Finding solutions (brainstorming, etc.)

    g. Writing agreements

    h. Other issues (remaining neutral, handling anger, group building, cooperation, affirmation)

  4. Ongoing mediator development

    a. Bias awareness, cultural diversity, prejudice reduction

    b. Power issues

    c. Practice difficult mediations

    d. Assertiveness

B. Length of Training

School-based mediation programs operate in a variety of different ways. Likewise, the training of mediators may vary to accommodate a particular school's schedule or the age and developmental level of the students. For example, a training for elementary students might be conducted in 1 1/2 hour sessions over a several week period, whereas a training for high school students might be done in full-day sessions over a one or two week period.

    The hours below reflect a minimum total of time for the particular age level. Length of session and span of time should be determined by the trainers in consultation with school staff. Some programs begin with conflict resolution training. These may fall at the lower end of the number of hours below:

  1. Elementary: 12–16 hours

  2. Middle School: 12–16 hours

  3. High School: 15–20 hours

  4. Follow-up: 2–10 hours

IX. Evaluation

It is essential to have an evaluation component to a school-based mediation program. Whenever possible, it is helpful to use outside evaluation (such as a university or the central administration office) for a school's program. It is important to know what you're trying to measure and take into consideration the school's concerns and the funding source's concerns in developing a plan for evaluation. Below are the areas that need to be covered in any evaluation of a school-based peer mediation program.

A. *Mediators*

Evaluating mediators takes place during training with debriefing of role-plays and activities. This should be ongoing with debriefing of mediators after the mediation session. Since this can be time consuming, here are some suggestions:

1. Self-evaluation checklist for mediators
2. Reporting back to coordinators through an "I need to talk" response for checking on the bottom of mediation report
3. Exit polls with disputants

B. *Program*

1. Pre- and post-test of trainees
2. School climate questionnaire
3. Analysis before and after program of discipline problems, incidents of fighting
4. Parent questionnaire

For further information about available curricula, specific programs, trainers, evaluation tools, and resources, please contact the NAME office at 413-545-2462.

APPENDIX A.6

≈ ≈

Conflict Resolution and Peer Mediation Organizations

The National Association for Community Mediation
1726 M Street NW, Suite 500
Washington, DC 20036-4502
Phone: 202-467-6226

The National Association for Mediation in Education/National Institute for Dispute Resolution
1726 M Street NW, Suite 500
Washington, DC 20036-4502
Phone: 202-466-4764 ext. 305

Wilmington College Peace Resource Center
Pyle Center
Box 1183
Wilmington, OH 45177

The Community Board Program
1540 Market St., Suite 490
San Francisco, CA 94102
Phone: 415-626-0595

Massachusetts Association of Mediation Programs and Practitioners
133 Federal St., 11th Floor
Boston, MA 02110-1703
Phone: 617-451-2093

The International Society of Professionals in Dispute Resolution
815 15th St. NW, Suite 530
Washington, DC 20005
Phone: 202-783-7277

Boston Area Educators for Social Responsibility
11 Garden St.
Cambridge, MA 02138

APPENDIX A.7

≈ ≈

Parent Permission Letter

_____, 199____

Dear Parent/Guardian of_____:

Congratulations, your child has volunteered and been selected to become trained as a peer mediator in the _____ Peer Mediation Program, which began in _____! A peer mediator's role is to help students resolve their disputes peacefully by cooperatively constructing a mutually satisfactory agreement. Enclosed is "Ten Reasons for Instituting a School-based Mediation Program" by Albie Davis and Kit Porter which tells why mediation is a positive learning experience for students.

The peer mediators added a new role for themselves last spring: peer helper. Any third-, fourth-, or fifth-grade student who wants to sit down and talk out a problem can fill out a request form and know that a peer helper will listen to his/her situation. A peer helper, like a peer mediator, _cannot_ give advice. However, by using mediator listening and restating skills, a peer helper guides the student in brainstorming ways to deal with the problem.

We are writing to ask permission to train your child as a member of the peer mediator/helper team. Training is scheduled . . . on (dates and times). Students will be excused from regular classes to participate in the training.

Beginning on (date), peer mediator/helpers will be required to attend a _weekly_ after-school session on (day) from (time) during which we will reinforce mediation skills through discussion and activities. This session will be designated as an "after-school program" as described in (the school's) Handbook.

On (day and time), an induction ceremony will be held in the auditorium. A brief reception for all peer mediator/helpers and their families will take place next to the auditorium following the ceremony. You are cordially invited to attend this wonderful event. Mediators will begin their duties with adult volunteers during lunch on a rotating schedule on that day.

Your child's participation as a mediator is voluntary, and he or she may withdraw from the program at any time.

If you have questions or concerns about this program, please call (coordinator's phone number). Our principal, (name), has also signed this letter to indicate that s/he is fully aware of the program and that s/he supports its continuation. We ask that you sign and return a copy of this letter to one of the coaches. Please keep the second copy for your records. Thank you.

Sincerely yours,

_____   _____
MEDIATION COORDINATOR   PRINCIPAL

_____   _____   _____
MEDIATION COACH   MEDIATION COACH   MEDIATION COACH

PLEASE READ AND SIGN

The purpose of this program has been explained to me and my child. I understand that his/her participation is voluntary and that he/she may exclude him/herself from the peer mediation/helper program at any time.

_____ Yes, I give my consent for my child to participate in the (school) Peer Mediation/Helper Program as a peer mediator/helper and attend the two-day training. She/he will attend the after-school program every (day and time).
_____ I will provide transportation.
_____ My child will ride the after-school bus.
_____ No, I do not want my child to participate in the (school) Peer Mediation/Helper Program as a peer mediator/helper.

_____   _____
SIGNATURE OF PARENT/GUARDIAN   DATE

_____ Yes, I want to participate in the (school) Peer Mediation/Helper Program as a peer mediator/helper and attend the two-day training and after-school program every (day and time).
_____ No, I do not want to participate in the (school) Peer Mediation/ Helper Program as a peer mediator/helper.

_____   _____
SIGNATURE OF STUDENT   DATE

We also NEED PARENTS to volunteer as adult supervisors during any one of the first or second lunch periods when mediations/peer helper sessions will be scheduled. PLEASE HELP US once a week by volunteering for a time slot below. Without an adult to supervise, we are unable to schedule peer mediators/helpers. Please join (coordinator) and several teachers as volunteers. (Coordinator) will meet with you and explain how to supervise the peer mediators/helpers if you check off "Yes" below.

_____ Yes, I would be interested in volunteering to supervise the peer mediators/helpers once a week. Please call me: _____
                                                      PHONE NUMBER
_____ No, I am not able to volunteer.

PLEASE CHECK OFF ANY TIMES THAT YOU WOULD BE AVAILABLE.

MONDAYS	TUESDAYS	WEDNESDAYS	THURSDAYS	FRIDAYS
10:30–11:15				
11:15–11:45				

PLEASE RETURN THIS PERMISSION LETTER BY (date).

REFERENCES

Bankier, P., Prod., and J. Dondlinger, Dir. 1991. *Peacemakers of the Future.* Amherst, MA: National Association for Mediation in Education. Videotape.

Benenson, W. 1988. Assessing the Effectiveness of a Peer Based Conflict Management Program in Elementary School. Ph.D. diss., University of Idaho. In *Dissertation Abstracts International*, 49, DA8819263.

Berthoff, A. E. 1981. *The Making of Meaning: Metaphors, Models, and Maxims for Writing Teachers.* Montclair, NJ: Boynton/Cook.

Bosworth, K. 1995. "Caring for Others and Being Cared for: Students Talk Caring in School." *Phi Delta Kappan*, 76 (9); 686–93.

Brown, R. G. 1991. *Schools of Thought: How the Politics of Literacy Shape Thinking in the Classroom.* San Francisco: Jossey-Bass.

Bruner, J. 1990. *Acts of Meaning.* Cambridge, MA: Harvard University Press.

Cahill, P. 1989. "Peer Mediation: Program Teaches Youngsters to Resolve Disputes Peacefully." *Union-News* (Greenfield, MA), February 13, Living section, p. 1.

Cahoon, P. 1987/1988. "Mediator Magic." *Educational Leadership*, 87 (4); 92–94.

Charney, B. R. 1991. *Teaching Children to Care: Management in the Responsive Classroom.* Greenfield, MA: Northeast Foundation for Children.

Cohen, R. 1987a. "School-Based Mediation Programs: Obstacles to Implementation." *NAME News*, 10; 1–4.

———. 1987b. "School Mediation Program Development: Implementation Checklist." *Setting Up a Program: General Packet.* Cambridge, MA: Richard Cohen/School Mediation Associates.

———. 1995. *Students Resolving Conflict: Peer Mediation in Schools.* Glenview, IL: GoodYear Books.

Coles, R. 1986. *The Moral Life of Children.* Boston: Houghton Mifflin.

———. 1993. *The Call of Service: A Witness to Idealism.* Boston: Houghton Mifflin.

Csikszentmihalyi, M. 1990. "Literacy and Intrinsic Motivation." *Daedalus: Journal of the American Academy of Arts and Sciences*, 119 (spring 1990): 115–40.

Davis, A., and K. Porter. 1985a. "Dispute Resolution: The 'Fourth R'". *Missouri Journal of Dispute Resolution*, 1985; 121–139.

———. 1985b. "Tales of Schoolyard Mediation." *Update on Law-Related Education*, 9 (1); 20–28.

Deutsch, M. 1982. *Conflict Resolution: Theory and Practice.* New York: Teachers College, Columbia University.

———. 1993. *Summary Report: The Effects of Training in Conflict Resolution and Cooperative Learning in an Alternative High School.* New York: Teachers College, Columbia University, International Center for Cooperation and Conflict Resolution.

Dewey, J. (1916) 1944. *Democracy and Education.* New York: Macmillan.

———. (1938) 1963. *Experience and Education.* New York: Macmillan.

Dreyfuss, E. T. 1990. "Learning Ethics in School-Based Mediation Programs." *Update on Law Related Education,* (Spring); 22–27.

Dreyfuss, E. T., A. Carter, and J. A. Zimmer. 1991. *The Conflict Management and Mediation Handbook.* Cleveland, OH: Cleveland-Marshall College of Law.

Ellsworth, M. A. 1993. Middle School Students Learning Language for Conflict Resolution in a Community in Conflict: A Book of Lessons or a Way of Being? Ph.D. diss., University of Iowa, Iowa City.

Erickson, F. 1982. "Taught Cognitive Learning in Its Immediate Environments: A Neglected Topic in the Anthropology of Education." *Anthropology & Education Quarterly,* 13; 149–80.

———. 1984. "What Makes School Ethnography 'Ethnographic'?" *Anthropology & Education Quarterly,* 15; 51–66.

Ferrara, J. 1994. Fourth- and Fifth-Grade Students as Problem Finders Within the Discourse of Mediation. Ph.D. diss., University of New Hampshire. In *Dissertation Abstracts International,* 55, DA9506413.

Fetterman, D. M. 1989. *Ethnography Step by Step.* Newbury Park, CA: Sage.

Finn, P. J. 1993. *Helping Children Learn Language Arts.* New York: Longman.

Fisher, R., W. Ury, and B. Patton. 1991. *Getting to Yes: Negotiating Agreement Without Giving In.* 2d ed. New York: Penguin.

Flood, J., J. Jensen, D. Lapp, and J. R. Squire. 1991. *Handbook of Research on Teaching the English Language Arts.* New York: Macmillan.

Franklin Mediation Service. 1991. *Mediator Training Manual.* Greenfield, MA: Franklin Mediation Services.

Gee, J. P. 1990. *Social Linguistics and Literacies: Ideology in Discourses.* New York: Falmer Press.

Gilmore, P., and A. A. Glatthorn, eds. 1982. *Children In and Out of School: Ethnography and Education.* Washington, DC: Center for Applied Linguistics.

Gilson, J. 1991. *Sticks and Stones and Skeleton Bones.* New York: Lothrop, Lee & Shepard.

Goffman, E. 1959. *The Presentation of Self in Everyday Life.* New York: Doubleday.

———. 1967. *Interaction Ritual: Essays on Face to Face Behavior.* New York: Anchor.

Goodlad, J. I. 1984. *A Place Called School: Prospects for the Future.* New York: McGraw-Hill.

Graves, D. H. 1983. *Writing: Teachers and Children at Work.* Portsmouth, NH: Heinemann.

———. 1994. *A Fresh Look at Writing.* Portsmouth, NH: Heinemann.

Halliday, M. A. K. 1975. *Learning How to Mean: Explorations in the Development of Language.* London: Edward Arnold.

Hamachek, D. E. 1988. "Evaluating Self-Concept and Ego Development Within Erikson's

Psychosocial Framework: A Formulation." *Journal of Counseling and Development,* 66; 354–60.

Hanisch, K. A., and P. J. Carnevale. 1987. Gender Differences in Mediator Behavior. Paper presented at annual convention of the American Psychological Association, New York. ERIC Document Reproduction Service No. ED 292 037.

Johnson, D. W., and R. T. Johnson. 1986. *Structured Controversy: Making Conflicts Constructive in the Classroom.* Amherst, MA: National Association for Mediation in Education.

———. 1991. *Teaching Children to Be Peacemakers.* Edina, MN: Interaction Book.

Johnson, D. W., R. T. Johnson, B. Dudley, and R. Burnett. 1992. "Teaching Students to Be Peer Mediators." *Educational Leadership,* 50 (1); 10–13.

Koch, M. S. 1986. "Schools Can Replace Gladiators with Mediators." *Education Week,* 28 (April).

Koch, M. S., and S. Miller. 1987. "Resolving Student Conflicts with Student Mediators." *Principal,* 66 (4); 59–62.

Kreidler, W. J. 1990. *Elementary Perspectives 1: Teaching Concepts of Peace and Conflict.* Cambridge, MA: Educators for Social Responsibility.

Lam, J. A. 1989a. *The Impact of Conflict Resolution Programs on Schools: A Review and Synthesis of the Evidence.* 2d ed. Amherst, MA: National Association for Mediation in Education.

———. 1989b. *School Mediation Program Evaluation Kit.* Amherst, MA: National Association for Mediation in Education.

Lane, P. S., and J. J. McWhirter. 1992. "A Peer Mediation Model: Conflict Resolution for Elementary and Middle School Children." *Elementary School Guidance & Counseling,* 27; 15–23.

Lipsitz, J. 1995. "Prologue: Why We Should Care About Caring." *Phi Delta Kappan,* 76 (9); 665–66.

Massachusetts Teachers Association. 1995. *MTA Today,* 26 (4); 18–19.

Meredith, N. 1987. "Resolving Conflict: Kids, Communication and Compromise." *Parenting,* (August); 63–66.

Meyer, D. 1990. *On-Going Training Activities for Student Mediators.* Tucson, AZ: OUR TOWN Family Center.

National Association for Mediation in Education (NAME). 1987. "Issues and Response." *NAME News,* 10 (Spring).

———. 1991. *Setting Up a Program: General Packet.* Washington, D.C.: NAME/NIDR.

Newkirk, T. 1989. *More Than Stories: The Range of Children's Writing.* Portsmouth, NH: Heinemann.

Noddings, N. 1984. *Caring: A Feminine Approach to Ethics and Moral Education.* Berkeley, CA: University of California Press.

———. 1988. "An Ethic of Caring and Its Implications for Instructional Arrangements." *American Journal of Education,* 96 (2); 215–30.

———. 1995. "Teaching Themes of Care." *Phi Delta Kappan,* 76 (9); 680–85.

Piaget, J. 1975. *The Development of Thought: Equilibration of Cognitive Structures.* New York: Viking.

Sadalla, G., M. Holmberg, and J. Halligan. 1990. *Conflict Resolution: An Elementary School Curriculum.* San Francisco, CA: The Community Board Program, Inc.

Satchel, B. B. 1992. Increasing Prosocial Behavior of Elementary Students in Grades K–6 Through a Conflict Resolution Management Program. Ed.D. Practicum, Nova University. ERIC Document Reproduction Service No. ED 347 607.

Schrumpf, F., D. Crawford, and H. C. Usadel. 1991. *Peer Mediation: Conflict Resolution in Schools Program Guide.* Champaign, IL: Research Press.

Shatles, D. 1992. *Conflict Resolution Through Children's Literature: Impact II.* New York: The Teachers Network. ERIC Document Reproduction Service No. ED 344 976.

Spindler, G., ed. 1988. *Doing the Ethnography of Schooling: Educational Anthropology in Action.* Prospect Heights, IL: Waveland Press.

Stuart, L. A. 1991. *Conflict Resolution Using Mediation Skills in the Elementary Schools.* Report No. CG 023 411. Charlottesville, VA. ERIC Document Reproduction Service No. ED 333 258.

Teasdale, S. 1984. *Mirror of the Heart: Poems of Sara Teasdale.* New York: Macmillan.

Townley, A. 1993. "Report to the Membership." *The Fourth R* (October/November), 1; 3–4.

Ury, W. 1991. *Getting Past No: Negotiating with Difficult People.* New York: Bantam.

Van Maanen, J. 1988. *Tales of the Field: On Writing Ethnography.* Chicago, IL: University of Chicago Press.

Vermillion, A. G. 1989. Perceptions of Public School Administrators on Conflict Resolution Education: A Descriptive, Comparative Study. Ph.D. diss., University of New Mexico. In *Dissertation Abstracts International,* 50, 06A.

Vygotsky, L. S. 1978. *Mind in Society: The Development of Higher Psychological Processes.* Cambridge, MA: Harvard University Press.

Welch, G. 1989. "How We Keep Our Playground from Becoming a Battlefield." *The Executive Educator,* 11 (5); 23, 31.

Wolcott, H. F. 1988. "'Problem Finding' in Qualitative Research." In *School and Society: Learning Content Through Culture.* H. Trueba and C. Delgado-Gaitan, eds. New York: Praeger.

————. 1990. *Writing Up Qualitative Research.* Newbury Park, CA: Sage.

Zemelman, S., H. Daniels, and A. Hyde. 1993. *Best Practice: New Standards for Teaching and Learning in America's Schools.* Portsmouth, NH: Heinemann.